Dramatic
Circumstances

On Acting,
Singing, and Living
Inside the Stories We Tell

William Wesbrooks

APPLAUSE
THEATRE & CINEMA BOOKS

An Imprint of
Hal Leonard Corporation

Published in 2014 by Applause Theatre & Cinema Books
An Imprint of Hal Leonard Corporation
7777 West Bluemound Road
Milwaukee, WI 53213

Trade Book Division Editorial Offices
33 Plymouth St., Montclair, NJ 07042

Printed in the United States of America

Book design by UB Communications

Library of Congress Cataloging-in-Publication Data

Wesbrooks, William.
    Dramatic circumstances : on acting, singing, and living inside the stories we tell / William Wesbrooks.
        pages cm
    ISBN 978-1-4768-2301-0
    1. Acting. I. Title.
    PN2061.W46 2014
    792.02'8—dc23
                                        2013050019

www.applausebooks.com

Dramatic
Circumstances

For Dallett,

as if
I ever had
another choice

CONTENTS

Once Upon a Time

I cannot remember a time in my life when I was not fascinated by singing and acting. In my earliest childhood fantasies, I wanted to be an actor. Actually, I wanted to be a movie star—not necessarily the same thing as being an actor, but close enough. I spent a lot of time singing and acting when I was in high school and college, and in the fall of 1973, I packed my life into two black metal foot-lockers and moved to New York to attend the American Academy of Dramatic Arts. Following my graduation from acting school, I was delighted to find that there were people out there in the world who were indeed willing to pay me money to sing and act. They did not pay me a lot of money, but it was validation nonetheless.

In the late 1970s I began directing, and it didn't take long for me to figure out that the role of "director" was the one I had always been meant to play. As a stage director, I found not only my first financial security in my chosen profession, meaning I no longer had to take work outside of the theatre, but also my first sense of fulfillment as an artist. As a director, I got to work one-on-one with singers and actors whose training and talent I respected and admired, and it was as a director that I first discovered the power inherent in a good story: how stimulating and satisfying it could be to tell each story by "living" inside it.

I agree wholeheartedly with the English author Philip Pullman, who said, "After nourishment, shelter and companionship, stories are the thing we need most in the world." Stories, I believe, are the most immediate way in which we as individuals and as a society come to perceive, and perhaps understand, the nature of human behavior and the complexities of human interaction. It was as a director that I felt myself fully immersed in the soul and substance of each story I got to tell, each show I got to direct.

After almost two decades of making my living as a director, I started teaching, and in the spring of 1999, I was hired as an adjunct instructor for an "acting for singers" course in the Steinhardt School at New York University. Two years later I was invited to become a member of NYU's full-time faculty and was appointed Director of Vocal Performance. I was given a mandate by the school to bring the students and teachers in both classical voice and music theatre together into one cohesive program, and as a person of the theatre who truly loved music and singing, I gave myself a mandate to bring together the study of singing and the study of acting in a way that would allow our students to commit fully to both disciplines.

I am now in my thirteenth year at NYU, and I am devoted more than ever to the training of young performers—who, I am very happy to find, are consistently determined to sing and act at the same time without compromising the integrity of either of these two demanding fields of study. I am keenly aware that my time in the Steinhardt School has been both the most rewarding and the most challenging time of my career. It has been rewarding to know and work with so many talented, committed people—students and teachers alike—as we examine every day the craft and the art of acting and singing. At the same time it has been a challenge to constantly explore and articulate the different ways my colleagues and I can most effectively inspire the best work in our students and ourselves. Every day in my work I get to show actors and singers how to create their stories and how to live inside them. Every day I am rewarded by getting to watch these young performers make tremendous changes as they become more adept at living truthfully inside each and every story they tell, and it is my work at NYU and my interaction with my students and my colleagues that have inspired me to write this book.

This book is intended to give you an experience similar to that of the students who spend a semester with me in one of my acting classes. The core work that I do with my students takes the form of a "coaching." A coaching is one singer, one accompanist, and me working through the story of a song and exploring the dramatic elements that will bring it to life. In order to demonstrate this process to you, I have recreated the coachings that best illustrate the concepts I think are the most important. The coaching transcripts presented in the book are actually amalgamations of different sessions with different students.

As you "observe" the coachings, I encourage you to take yourself through the process along with each of the performers. That is what I ask my students to do when they are observing the work of another student. Answer for yourself the questions that are being asked, and make the choices that feel right for you. When you approach each of the coachings as if you yourself were singing that song, I think you will discover that your sense of the story and your place in it will become increasingly clear.

This book is about stories and it is, in turn, made up of stories. It is about the way we in the theatre go about telling our stories and how we, when we perform, can choose to live inside the stories we tell. It is a book about why stories matter, both to us as we tell them and to those who hear them. Most importantly, it is a book about how you can learn to live inside each and every story you tell and, as a result, reap the many rewards of being someone who is able to do so.

Philip Pullman also said, "'Thou shalt not' might reach the head, but it takes 'Once upon a time' to reach the heart." It is my sincere hope that the stories in this book—some of my favorite "Once upon a times"—reach your heart.

William Wesbrooks
January 2014

Putting It Together

If you are a student of singing and acting, your study is made up of many separate parts—the bits and pieces of information that you glean from many different teachers in different areas of study. The goal is to take those separate parts and bring them together into a unified whole: a fully realized presentation of yourself and your material that you—and your teachers—hope will "have it all." For students of singing and acting, it is all about, as Stephen Sondheim so eloquently expresses in *Sunday in the Park with George*, "putting it together."

And just how do you do that? That is the challenge. That is the very thing that I find is rarely taught and often not even discussed. But as a theatre person in a music program, I have, for the past decade, had no choice but to "put it together," and my experience in doing that very thing is what inspired me to write this book.

My voice-teacher colleagues and I spend many hours each year auditioning singers who want to study in our program. It is not at all unusual for us to hear a young singer with a very good instrument who is singing inefficiently. For example, a young woman might be singing too loudly, with too much pressure, or in a vocal adjustment too far back in her throat that keeps the sound from moving freely throughout the full range of her voice. When we hear this kind of functional problem, we usually take the time to find out if the singer can make vocal adjustments that will address one or more of these issues. One of us might say, "Place the words at the very tip of your tongue, as if they were being formed right behind your teeth." In almost every instance when a singer does that, the voice will move at least some degree forward. One of my voice-teacher colleagues might have the young woman sing a line or two on a lip trill in order to get her air moving more evenly, and another might just ask her to sing more softly in order to take off pressure. As the acting teacher in the room, I might ask the singer to imagine she is rocking a restless baby in a cradle, and the result of her taking that action and telling that story is often that the resonance will move forward, there will be less pressure in the vocal production, and the air will flow more freely and evenly.

Why does this happen? It happens because in taking on the role of someone who needs to quiet a restless baby, the singer will naturally focus on the baby. As she does that, her words will become more important. They will be articulated more carefully and will likely move "forward" in her mouth, bringing her sound out of her throat. Because she is trying to soothe her imaginary baby, she will probably sing more softly, thus backing off on the pressure and allowing her air to flow more gently and evenly. The most valuable lesson to be learned here, however, is that when this young woman's job becomes taking care of the baby rather than singing well for the audition panel, her natural instincts and more efficient vocal function will naturally come into play.

Does this example demonstrate that approaching a singer from an acting perspective is more effective than addressing each specific vocal issue? In fact, it does not mean that at all. All good teachers, whether they teach singing or acting, understand that the myriad skills that come together to make a unified "voice" need to be addressed from different perspectives. If you are fortunate enough to study with voice teachers and acting teachers who address the components of your work with a shared aesthetic and vocabulary, you will find yourself more readily able to understand and implement the various ways of working that will best lead you to your own voice. And if you are truly blessed and study with teachers who actually take the time and make the effort to have these conversations with each other, your journey to your own voice will be much more efficient and a lot more fun.

Working as closely as I do with my voice-teacher colleagues, I have learned some very important things about singing and acting—things I wish I had known back when I was in school and trying so hard to find my own voice. These things are:

- Thoughtful preparation that includes a deep connection to breath is the conduit through which singers can unlock not only their voices but also the songs themselves and the stories those songs are meant to tell.
- The understanding of and adherence to a healthy vocal technique need never interfere with a singer's impulse to take a fully committed and realized action.
- Fully committed actions and the emotional connections that may arise from those actions need never compromise a singer's access to a vocal technique being carefully acquired and thoughtfully maintained.

There are two premises that form the foundation of the work I do with singers and actors. The first is that truthful acting does not require that singers sacrifice healthy vocal production. The second is that good singing does not require that singers close themselves off from what they feel. For more than a decade, I have seen it demonstrated time and time again that the thing that brings a singer's acting and singing together as a whole, the thing that makes these two premises not only true but extremely powerful, is the full use of breath inspired by a strong connection to a character's intention. Breath and intention are the keys that unlock all doors.

Whether you are speaking, singing, or taking a physical action, truthful behavior always is and *always must be* inspired by intention. By acquiring an empathetic knowledge of the fundamental nature of human behavior, singers and actors can learn to identify the wants and needs that inspire the actions they take. They can learn to recognize, name, and connect to the true source of their intentions, and as they learn how to do that, they will be able to utilize the power of those intentions to propel themselves into behavior. Behavior, for the purposes of this book, is made up of the acting and singing actions that performers must take in response to the compelling nature of their wants and needs. This is true in performance, and as is so often the case for performers, it is also true in life.

I want to take a moment here to acknowledge that for the purposes of this book, I have not included dance in the conversation. It is not that I think that the same principles do not apply. I believe that they absolutely do. Performers face the same communication challenges when it comes to movement and dance as they do when it comes to acting and singing. Dance, however, is the area about which I have the least amount of practical information to offer, and it is a discipline about which I do not feel qualified to write. I want to keep the work we are doing as simple and straightforward as possible. This work and this way of thinking about your work will certainly have an impact on the way you move. It can change the way you connect to your body and the way you allow an impulse to inspire any physical action. However, the process whereby a physical action is heightened to a level of dance by the performer's need to move is not something I am going to explore in this book.

This book is about what you as a student of acting and singing need to do to satisfy the highest standards for both of these demanding disciplines and to meet those standards while practicing both disciplines at the same time. If the foundation of the actor's craft begins with a full and free breath, and if the action that takes place on the exhale is informed by a free release of that breath, then the processes of acting and singing can, and will, nourish each other. Rather than trying to serve two masters at the same time, there is in reality only one master to be served. That master is you—the you that is discovered through exploring the honest impulses that derive from your ability to live inside every story you choose to tell.

1
Suitable for All Ages

When I was a young child, my family often spent the Christmas holidays with my grandparents, aunts, uncles, and cousins in the little house in Kansas where my father grew up. In the evenings, the grownups would sit in the living room talking, while the children, ranging from about age four to age nine, would play together in a large room off the back porch that was always referred to as "the bunkhouse." One of our favorite games was an elaborate version of "house." Everyone would be assigned a role, and we would go about our daily routine interacting in ways that I assume reflected what went on in our individual households. The "dads" would go to work while the "moms" stayed home and the "children" went to school. The "family" would then come back together to fix dinner or clean house or go on a picnic.

One evening we decided to give our make-believe family a baby—that role being assumed by one of the many stray dolls lying about the room. No sooner had the baby entered the picture than someone decided it was sick. A "doctor" was summoned who gave the baby many pills, and because children are basically sadistic in nature, the baby also had to endure a series of painful injections. Then someone had a better idea: "What if the baby died?" And the moment that question was asked, our game of "house" turned into a game of "funeral," complete with a makeshift coffin, church pews, and a preacher.

About that time, our actual mothers in the front part of the house decided they had better go see what the children were up to. They came back to the bunkhouse and opened the door, only to find all of us singing a hymn and most of us in tears. The immediate mom reaction—the natural mom reaction to a crying child—was to find out who had done what to whom. They asked what was wrong, and in virtually one voice we cried out, "The baby died!" The crying intensified, along with our mothers' confusion, and while I do not remember exactly what happened next, I know it was quite some time before everyone got calmed down and packed off to bed.

Why am I telling you this story? I am telling you this story because I believe it illustrates the underlying premise of this book: playing the "what if" game can have a profound impact on your imagination, your behavior, and your ability to live inside any story that you decide to tell. The tale of the bunkhouse also supports something else that I feel is of vital importance to anyone who wants to be a performer: the best performers, no matter their age, are willing and able to play as if they were still very young children.

The wants and needs of young children live at the forefront of their experience, and every day, children devote most of their time and energy to getting those wants and needs fulfilled. Children know what it is to win and what it is to lose, and they will keep trying to win even when it appears the odds are against them. When they win they are happy, and when they lose they are not.

When children are getting their way they can be kind and loving, and when thwarted they can be unpleasant and cause no end of trouble. There is just no question that children are born actors and that they know how to play.

I am not a psychologist, but I do know that playing is an essential way children prepare themselves for adulthood. It is through play that they begin to incorporate a wide array of life's experiences into their perceptions of what things are and what they mean. Play is a mental, physical, and emotional exercise that is as critical to a child's well-being and healthy development as plenty of sleep and good nutrition. In their July 19, 2010, *Newsweek* article "The Creativity Crisis," psychologists and researchers Po Bronson and Ashley Merryman reported the following:

> Preschoolers who spend more time in role-play (acting out characters) have higher measures of creativity: voicing someone else's point of view helps develop their ability to analyze situations from different perspectives. When playing alone, highly creative [children] may act out strong negative emotions: they'll be angry, hostile, anguished. The hypothesis is that play is a safe harbor to work through forbidden thoughts and emotions.

The "what if the baby died" game my cousins and I decided to play was a safe way for us to explore the idea of death, and the game derived its power from our ability as children to both create a story about death and live inside that story. At the point in my life when my cousins and I decided to play that particular game, I had never been to a funeral. There had been no recent deaths in our extended family, and like most children, we had little experience of death, no real sense of what it would mean to die. But we were children. We saw the world in simpler terms, and we felt no sense of limitation imposed by the fact that these were things we had not actually experienced. We were wholly committed to pretending. We knew the funeral was only a game and that nothing in our "what if" was real. There was no baby. There was no funeral. There was only our commitment to behaving as if those things existed, *as if* they were real. Thus, something that was not *real* became nonetheless, in our young minds, *true*.

The thing that we, as children, could readily do was commit completely to our belief in a story while knowing full well that the story was taking place only in our imaginations. Our "funeral" game allowed us—actually required us—to access and occupy our imaginations in such a way that the line between actual events and imagined events became blurred. By the time our mothers walked into the room, we did not quite know the difference between what was real and what was make-believe. Furthermore, we did not care. We were playing a game, and at some level we still knew it was a game, even as we became increasingly distraught.

In *Alice's Adventures in Wonderland*, Lewis Carroll shows us that Alice's favorite phrase is "Let's pretend." In his article on *Alice in Wonderland*, "Rabbit Redux," published in *Newsweek* (March 8, 2010), Ramin Setoodeh points out that what Alice also does is "remind us how little we do that anymore." Setoodeh writes, "The only way to understand Alice is to use your imagination. Do you even remember how to do that?...The genius of the 145-year-old *Wonderland* is that it forces you to bring your creative juices to the tea party."

But don't grownups still enjoy games of make-believe? They absolutely do. They read stories or watch them on television. They go to the theatre and the movies. The critical difference, however, between a child's enjoyment of make-believe and that of most adults is that most adults prefer to observe their stories from the outside. For children, that is just not enough. Children want to take part. They want to step into every story and take an active role in making the events of that story come to life, and they somehow manage to do that even if they sit still throughout the telling of the story. In other words, just like grownup performers who want to live inside the stories they tell, children want to act!

Why do children want, even need, to act? The best answer to the "why" question is also the most significant. Children play games of make-believe first and foremost because it is fun. It is their favorite way to entertain themselves, and I think that the main reason young children are able to play so freely is because it does not really occur to them that anyone else is watching. They play for their own amusement, for their own benefit.

I do wish that there were, at this point, a way to avoid the term "inner child." The idea that we all have a childhood version of ourselves residing inside our adult psyches is a relevant view of human psychology that has, unfortunately, become the well-deserved butt of any number of jokes. For example, my all-time favorite faux self-help title, and winner of the word competition that ran for many years on the back page of *New York Magazine*, is *Kickboxing Your Inner Child*. Nonetheless, I firmly believe that a grownup who really wants to sing and act must seek, and then celebrate, the child inside—the child that still wants, needs, and knows how to play. I believe that it is by accessing that younger, less inhibited part of themselves that grownups can begin to experience the freedom and fun that comes with working from a fully engaged imagination.

There are myriad benefits available to those performers who commit to living inside their stories. These benefits include spontaneity in their actions, clarity in their intentions, and immediacy in their emotional responses. The challenge that most performers face (except for those who never really grew up in the first place) is how to go about finding their way to that world of make-believe into which children appear to have innate and ready access. The instructions "Relax! Have fun! Let yourself go!" may sound easy enough—the words do make for a nice song lyric—but for most of the performers I work with, it is not a matter of "letting go." It is a matter of "getting in."

Whenever I have the opportunity to observe young children, I am often struck by their apparent ability to move through life as if nothing in the world exists that is not about them. Therefore, their reaction to any event that might come their way, be it an invitation to play or an instruction to pick up their toys and get ready for bed, is always filtered through the perspective that there is no one else in the world who matters but them, and there is nothing else happening in the world except the events that are going to have an immediate impact on them. Not only are children the central characters of their own lives, but they also see themselves as the central characters of the lives of any other people whose paths may somehow cross theirs. This quality of self-absorption can make them frequently hard to live with, but always fascinating to observe.

The socializing process that we as children must eventually go through, however essential to society's expectations and a parent's sanity, is largely a matter of making us conscious of the fact that the world does not revolve only around us. But what is so often lost in that socializing process is our ability to experience ourselves as the center of even our own lives. Every story somehow becomes someone else's story in which we play only a secondary role. We become aware of how we are observed by those around us and become, unfortunately, overly conscious of how often we are watched and judged. That is, I believe, how we as adults disconnect from our innate ability to occupy stories in such an intensely personal and immediate way. The focus of the work I do with actors and singers is to help them reconnect to that ability.

If children are able to live out their stories so fully because for them the rest of the world does not exist, then grownups, I believe, have to take steps to make the rest of the world disappear—or at the very least, allow it to move into the background. I have found that the most effective way for performers to reach the "inside" of their stories is to take specific steps by which they can place themselves in a world of their own invention, a world in which the things they think, want, and feel are the only things that matter. Once again, simply watching a story unfold will not be enough. Like the children they used to be, they will have no choice but to be a part of the action, and doing that not only frees them in their work but also nourishes their spirits. Just as children learn about life from the games they play, these performers will learn so much about who they are and what they are able to do.

The dramatic circumstance process places you at the very center of your story, creates in you a strong need, focuses you on the most likely way to meet that need, and sets you off in pursuit of the thing you must have. The process is made up of a series of specific steps that will allow you to create the best, most potent stories and begin to live inside those stories as if they were taking place in the here and now.

You begin the process by identifying the story you want to tell. Within the context of that story, you articulate your *problem*, your *other*, and your *objective*. Once you have articulated these story elements in a vocabulary that resonates with your own life and experience, you have in hand a working dramatic circumstance. You take yourself through a physical preparation process that connects your breath and body to the elements of your circumstance, and that is how you will be able to occupy the story you are going to tell. From inside your story you will experience the impulse to take action, and once you have taken action, you will be able to play out your story as a person in pursuit of something that must be attained at all costs. You will be able to utilize the power and momentum that is inherent in any well-structured story.

Allowing yourself to explore a daring "what if" and act out the resulting story is, at the very least, a fun game to play. At its best it is a game that can empower you as a performer, and a person, in ways that you may not have previously imagined were possible. Like so many really good games, "what if" is easy to learn and can take a lifetime to perfect. As you spend time practicing, you will naturally become a better player. Each of your stories will get clearer and stronger, and the need that the story spurs inside you will compel you to take action. Fueled by your need, you will experience how truly liberating it can be to pursue an objective without worrying about how you are going to do it or—more importantly—how *well* you are doing it. You will begin to lose sight of the fact that you are being watched, and how fun is that?

Stanislavski described acting as living truthfully within an imaginary circumstance. In all my years of directing and teaching, I have never encountered an actor or singer who was not committed to living truthfully in the work he or she was doing, and I have no doubt that you share that same level of commitment. You want your work to be honest. You want your audience to believe you, and you know that in order to do that, you have to believe yourself.

How are you able to live truthfully in your work? You live truthfully by recognizing that it is your job to tell a story with every song you sing and, to the best of your ability, to live inside every story you tell. You make the story *your* story, and you take fully committed actions in order to get the things your characters want and need as if those wants and needs were your own.

Stanislavski, so eminently wise and quotable, also said that the word *if* "acts as a lever to lift us out of the world of actuality into the realm of imagination." Subsequently, "What if I were...?" is the question you must ask yourself as you set out to bring any story to life. It is a question that will spark your imagination and place you at the center of your story.

Thus, if you were preparing the role of Kim in *Miss Saigon*, you might ask yourself, "What if I were abandoned by the man I love and left all alone with the responsibility of raising our child in circumstances that were so dire and dangerous as to be life threatening?" The actor playing Anthony in *Sweeney Todd* could ask himself, "What if I were wandering through the streets of a strange city and suddenly encountered a girl so beautiful that I fell instantly in love, and even though she appeared to be out of reach, I knew in that instant that I would do anything I had to in order to spend the rest of my life with her?"

"What if I were...?" is the foundation of any number of approaches to acting that are based on getting an actor to identify an objective and focus on the pursuit of that objective. It is how you find your motivation—why you do the things you are going to do—and it makes clear to you what your objective must be. Playing the "what if" game is how you find out at any time and in any story just what it is you have to do. It is the starting place for a way of working that I have found to be very effective for actors in general and singers in particular.

Why is the "what if" game effective for actors? Acting is about doing things—literally taking action. It is essential that you keep in mind that acting is *not* about thinking things or feeling things. "What if" stimulates your imagination by asking you to explore a story that then reveals to you, as the main character of that story, what you must accomplish. Thus, your character's quest becomes your quest. Simply stated, playing the "what if" game helps you quit worrying and start *doing*.

Why is the "what if" game effective for singers in particular? It is effective for singers because it will allow you to immerse yourself in your stories in a manner that will not interfere with your singing. This process will, in fact, support your singing. You will learn much more about this aspect of the dramatic circumstance process in the pages that follow. For now, I will tell you that the secret lies in the way you breathe, the way you organize your thoughts, and the way you occupy the story you are telling.

Is it really that simple? Like most things in life, it is that simple and that complicated at the same time. Some students even experience this work as being *too* simple. It does not feel as if they are doing enough—as if they are even doing anything. At the same time, however, the students who express these concerns will often report that as they immerse themselves in their dramatic circumstances and utilize their commitment to their stories to focus their thoughts on the things they need to accomplish, everything around them appears to fade into the background. Technical and vocal concerns seem to take care of themselves. Transitions into various tactics or behaviors come quite naturally and require no conscious adjustments. The sense of emotional connection is both immediate and profound. They suddenly feel, in a word, *free*.

Freedom in performance is the goal of every singer and actor. When you are able to perform more freely, you are able to have more fun. The reverse is also true. The more fun you are having, the freer you are going to be. I believe that those two things together can inspire your most powerful work. When you are able to play in all of your stories like a child completely immersed in your own game of make-believe—no matter how serious the circum-stances and whether you are dealing with a dead baby or not—I promise that, just like my crying cousins and me back in the bunk-house, you will be having a rollicking good time.

2

Pieces of the Puzzle

Seaman Knapp was a turn-of-the-century educator who believed strongly in the practical application of scientific principles. He said many intelligent and insightful things throughout the course of his life, but Dr. Knapp is most often quoted as saying, "What a man hears, he may doubt. What he sees, he may possibly doubt. What he does himself, he cannot doubt."

There is no "doubt" in my mind that singing and acting are learn-by-doing activities. The only way to "get it" is to "do it." And once you have done it—once you have actually had the experience of taking a fully committed action and expressing yourself with a satisfying level of vocal and dramatic freedom—you will not doubt for a minute that an event of some significance has taken place. From that point forward, you will naturally seek that same experience each and every time you perform.

It is your job to *do it*, and it is your teacher's job to assist you. Those of us who work with singers and actors have borrowed the word *coach* from the training of athletes, and I think it is a good word to describe the way in which performers and their teachers most often work together. Your acting and singing teachers, like coaches, guide you from the sidelines as you commit yourself to the "game" you are playing. Your coaches are there to help you play your game to the best of your ability, but you are always the one who is making choices and decisions. You are the one doing the work. No coach, acting teacher, voice teacher, musical director, or stage director can play the game for you, nor, at the end of the day, can they play your game as well as you can.

And why is that? It is because regardless of the influence of any teacher, or the impact he or she may have on your work, you will always, in the final analysis, speak and act in what is uniquely *your own voice*. Finding that voice and allowing it to grow and evolve is the ultimate goal of anyone who embarks on the serious study of singing and acting. Too often I see performers trying to figure out who they are supposed to be rather than committing to a process that allows them to discover who, in fact, they are. Your own voice, the thing that is you and you alone, is the key, and it is the thing that all performers—all artists—are ultimately seeking.

What exactly is "your own voice"? Simply stated, your own voice is you. It is the entirety of you communicating from a place of freedom—complete, uninhibited, and unencumbered freedom. It has been my experience that performers will begin to discover that kind of freedom as they acquire a consistent and dependable level of skill in four specific areas.

- *Vocal freedom* is achieved when your instrument functions at its optimum level, thus allowing you full access to your complete range of vocal expression.
- *Mental freedom* is achieved when you are able to engage your imagination and fully explore any story without judging either the characters or yourself.

- *Physical freedom* is achieved as your body responds imme-diately to any physical or emotional impulse, allowing you to take a clear and fully realized action.
- *Emotional freedom* is achieved when you believe in your story to such an extent that you are able to live inside that story as if it were happening to you in that very time and place.

An ideal state of complete, uninhibited, and unencumbered ex-pression is something we all strive for in our work, and the degree of freedom we experience in any given moment is a product of the level of freedom we have been able to achieve in each of these four distinct, yet obviously interconnected, areas. You cannot have one without the other. It is important to keep in mind, however, that achieving freedom in these areas takes practice and patience. The freedom you seek is not, and never will be, an absolute. It will always be a matter of degree, and it will always be relative.

Relative to what? Relative to how free you were the last time you performed. You are not seeking perfection. Perhaps a better way to say this is that you are seeking perfection but not beating yourself up when you don't achieve it. What you can realistically pursue is the greatest level of freedom you are capable of achieving at any given moment when you are called upon to express yourself as an actor and singer.

Two for the Price of One

If you are like most people who decide to pursue a career perform-ing as a singer and actor, the process of discovering and owning your own voice can easily become your life's vocation. It requires years of study and practice. One of the many things that makes this work so challenging, while at the same time so satisfying, is that the "voice" you are seeking is an amalgamation of the literal and the figurative. Your path to freedom requires that you appreciate, study, and explore—and ultimately understand—both the literal and figurative aspects of yourself and your instrument.

What is the distinction between the literal and the figurative? Your *literal voice* is the product of the physical function of your vocal apparatus. It is the actual sounds you make when air moves through your vocal folds, causing them to vibrate at particular frequencies and with a particular resonance. Your articulators—your lips, tongue, teeth, palate, and jaw—shape those sounds into words that are either spoken or sung. The optimum function of your literal voice involves achieving your most efficient and consistent coordination of muscle and air. Singers and their teachers spend years, even lifetimes, exploring the intricacies of this amazing, uniquely human ability to communicate with a seemingly endless array of words and sounds. Some singers and teachers can get so caught up in perfecting the literal that they forget the figurative is at least equally, if not more, important.

Your *figurative voice* is what you have to say. Specifically, it is *why* you have to say it. It is the thing inside you that inspires the thoughts that cause you to take action. In life, that action is anything you say or do. In performance, that action is, for the most part, speaking and singing. Your figurative voice is ultimately shaped by how you see yourself and how you want others to see you, and just like your literal voice, it is the product of your genetics, environment, upbringing, education, values, desires, fears, thoughts, feelings, and beliefs. It is made up of everything that is you.

It is a performer's lifelong challenge to consistently bring the literal voice and the figurative voice together into a unified whole.

That is how through the songs you sing you will reveal yourself to your audience, whoever your audience may be, as a "whole" person in whatever state of being that person happens to be at that particular moment.

The Art of Singing

As a singer, you are, and always will be, a craftsperson. You are a craftsperson in the sense that you must develop and maintain a detailed working knowledge of your instrument—as well as the necessary skills you need to consistently access that instrument— that will provide you with many years of happy, healthy singing. You are a craftsperson, but you are also an artist.

What does it mean to be an artist? It means that you are a person who seeks to express your knowledge, your perspective, and your experience of life through the creation of work in which you call upon your talents to reveal and illuminate for the viewer, or the listener, fundamental human experiences that we all share and with which we can all identify. This is true if you sing in a choir or if you sing a solo in church. It is true if you perform in a school show, become the vocalist in a band, or study for a professional career. It is true if your hard work and effort have brought you some success and you have the great good fortune to be someone who is paid to sing in front of other people. It is even true if you sing in the shower for no particular reason, just because you feel like singing.

Whatever the place and time may be, when you sing, you are expressing your experience of life. That is, I believe, the main reason we like to do it, and it is also the main reason people like to hear it. Good singing—singing that is unencumbered by either vocal malfunction or artifice—reminds people of who they are. It reminds them what it means to be alive.

Whenever and wherever you sing, you are expressing what it is to be you. You are, at the same time, expressing what it is to be human. When you are able to do that truthfully and consistently, you will allow your audience to see inside your own particular world, whether that world is one you actually inhabit or one you have created in order to bring a character to life and tell that character's story. Whenever you are able to reveal the humanity of the person singing the song, an audience is able to recognize who that person is. More to the point, they recognize themselves in the person you are revealing to them. That is, I believe, an art.

Acting the Songs You Sing

Acting a song means bringing the singer of the song to life—fully and truthfully to life—in such a way that the listener believes that the words are actually yours: that the song is being "written" at the very moment it is being sung. Whenever you see and hear people sing songs, don't you know immediately whether or not you believe them? Don't you know, without even taking time to think about it, whether or not the words ring true? Whether or not the singer seems to believe the things that he or she is saying? Whether the singer is actually committed to the circumstance of the song or simply giving a performance that is meant to appear as if there is truth behind the words?

Making your words resonate truthfully is the goal to set for yourself every time you begin work on a piece of dramatic material. That may sound like a pretty tall order, but it is quite doable, and it is the challenge that faces you with every song you sing. It is the same challenge whether you are singing as yourself or singing as a character that you have chosen to play. The dramatic circumstance process provides a method with which you can meet that challenge successfully for every song you choose to sing, no matter the genre or venue or when you are called upon to sing the song.

Dramatic Circumstances

Acting, the way I have come to view it and for the purposes of the process I teach, is a game in which you explore and expand your experience of life by taking a walk in someone else's shoes. It is a game in which you allow yourself to move for a moment into someone else's life, thus allowing yourself to behave as if you were in that person's circumstance. You, the principal player of the game, envision yourself in a broad array of life-inspired situations, and you take action based on those things you envision. The circumstances and behaviors you explore encompass both the good situations that life may bring and the not-so-good situations that life so often brings. It is, in case you have not discovered this already, the not-so-good situations that are usually more dramatic and always more interesting.

How do you play the game? You play the game by engaging your imagination. You imagine yourself in a dramatic circumstance, and you then take specific steps that allow you to occupy that circumstance. It is your successful occupation of a circumstance that will compel you to take action—to act.

How do you engage your imagination? You engage your imagination by engaging your brain and creating in your mind a story that is rich with danger, romance, adventure, and possibility. The point is that you create a dramatic story in which you are the central character. You cast yourself in the leading role.

A broken heart has certainly been the impetus for many a good song, and if you are singing a song with a "broken-heart circumstance," you might ask yourself, "What if I were left standing at the altar by the person I love with all my heart and with whom I thought I was going to spend the rest of my life?" You would envision and explore that situation in the context of your own life experience: your thoughts about love and commitment, your memories of someone you have loved, your knowledge of someone you love now, your fantasies of someone you may someday love—or who may someday love you. It is through a process of envisioning and exploring your needs, wants, and desires that you will find yourself able to tap into a powerful source of expression that lives at the very center of your being.

What is it again that lies at the very center of your being? At the core of your being there is a confluence of knowledge, feeling, and need. It is a source of power that resides in the core of every person on the planet. You are going to use your imagination to access and utilize that power.

And what does all this mean? It means that the study of acting is also the study of self.

Your ability to act is inherently linked to your ability to empathize: to understand and share the experiences of another person. You cannot truly appreciate what another person is going through unless you acknowledge and articulate the things you yourself have gone through. It is this development of an empathetic nature that will allow you to most effectively occupy the circumstances that confront the characters you may play. It is what will make you an honest actor.

Why does all this matter? Learning to fully engage your imagination and experience the sense of freedom that can result from that engagement is a deeply satisfying activity. I believe that an honest examination of life's experiences is the soul and substance of the study of acting, and I also believe that it is the principal benefit that the acting game has to offer. This benefit—this opportunity to know and express yourself—is available to you regardless of your age or your background. It is available to you regardless of whether or not your ultimate desire is to perform in front of other people.

What determines if you will be any good at this acting game? Your fundamental willingness to give it a try.

3
Making Each Story
Your Own

I want to begin this chapter by emphasizing what I said in the last chapter.

> Acting a song means bringing the singer of the song to life—fully and truthfully to life—in such a way that the listener believes that the words are actually yours: that the song is being "written" at the very moment it is being sung.

How do you become the "writer" of every song you sing? You do that by making the story of every song you sing your own story. That will inspire you to behave in ways that reveal to your audience just who the person is that is living inside that story. You know what they say: "Actions speak louder than words." Nothing could be truer for performers who are trying to tell their stories and bring characters to life in front of an audience. Your actions speak louder than your words, and it is in taking those actions that you will reveal who you are.

The actions that are always the most revealing are those that people take when they are under pressure, because the way people behave under pressure often reveals the truth of who they are. When people are under pressure and focusing on what needs to get done rather than how well they are doing it, they are less able to conceal their thoughts, feelings, and intentions. We are able to see through to the very things that their behavior is designed to conceal. Keep in mind that one of the most fun things about performing is that acting truthfully does not have to mean telling the truth.

The story you occupy will force you to take action to get something you want, and striving to achieve that objective will put you under pressure in a couple of different ways. There is pressure in knowing that you might fail, and there is pressure in knowing that as you are forced to reveal what you want and what you are willing to do to get it, you will have no choice but to lower your defenses, thus becoming more vulnerable. The point, and the good news for the actor, is that whenever you set out to accomplish something that really matters to you, you are going to be at risk. Putting yourself at risk is the most effective way to get yourself to live more fully inside your story.

Whenever you perform, what you need to do will always be clear as long as what your character wants to achieve is clear. Your pursuit of what your character wants—your objective—will be fueled by your need to get whatever that thing is that is so important to you, and you will do everything in your power to get it. You will be driven and inspired by your determination to win. Many people would even argue that the measure of an actor's talent relates directly to what that actor is able to do—and willing to do—in order to win.

The actions that you take while under pressure are going to reveal things about you. Your audience will be able to see what you care about, who you love, and what you are willing to do in order to get the things you want and need. Your commitment to winning will leave you no choice but to utilize your strength of purpose, your imagination, your humor, your intelligence, your compassion, your courage—all of those things that audiences want to see when they step into a world being brought to life for them by a good actor. These things, these attributes of inspired actions and behavior, are how an audience comes to "know" a character and identify with characters as they watch them behave.

One important point of clarification: there is a difference between putting yourself *as the character* under pressure and putting yourself *as the performer* under pressure. To work most effectively and freely as an actor and singer, you must always be able to access your breath and the full function of your physical instrument in spite of the fact that your character may well be experiencing a significant degree of stress. Achieving a balance between using the pressure of your story to fuel your behavior and not letting that energy knock your instrument out of efficient function is one of the aspects of a performer's training that takes the most time. You must be mindful of this balance as you learn how to draw energy from a character's need and commitment, without letting that energy impede your performer's ability to speak and sing. Quoting again the ever-dependable Stanislavski: "At times of great stress it is especially necessary to achieve a complete freeing of the muscles."

It is the need, risk, and determination of your character that you must explore and utilize in your work. When as an actor you are able to approach your dramatic circumstance from the perspective of your character's need, risk, and determination, you will actually be liberating yourself as an actor.

Why is that? Because you will be turning your energy and focus to the solving of a problem instead of distracting yourself by trying to be good, sing right, get the job, or impress the audience—any of the many things that can derail you in performance. By focusing on what your character must accomplish, you will be taking charge of your work in a new way, and in that taking charge you will be empowering yourself.

Actors are meant to "behave" in front of their audiences, and really good actors behave in such a way that their audiences feel as if they know the people they are watching. The audience recognizes and empathizes with the behavior they observe, and they then identify with the character you are bringing to life for them. That is the route by which an audience comes to care about the story and the character they are watching. By natural transference, they also come to care about you, the person they are actually watching. That is the kind of acting you want to do and the kind of actor you want to be. And you accomplish that by analyzing your situation, identifying the conflict, and organizing your thoughts in a way that will put your character at the greatest risk. You place yourself in the middle of a conflict-ridden situation, and using that situation as your source material, you identify the elements of your dramatic circumstance. Creating your circumstance and then stepping inside it is what will propel you into action and, in the work we are doing now, make you sing your song.

Start at the Beginning

The simplest way to describe the process whereby you explore and articulate your dramatic circumstance is to say that for each song you sing, you are going to tell a story—a story in which you are the main character. That story will be constructed in such a way that it will lead you, as the story's central character, to a point of crisis. When you reach that point of crisis, you will have no choice but to take an action, because that action will be the only way in which you can overcome the crisis moment, achieve your objective, and give your story a happy ending. You do not always get a happy ending, but you must always try for one.

Let's "write" a story and then take the elements of that story to devise a potent dramatic circumstance.

I recently completed the annual process of selecting participants for a summer music theatre workshop at NYU. While sitting at my computer one afternoon, I started thinking about the many applicants, their audition videos, and everything the applicants were probably hoping for when they submitted those videos. That got me to thinking about a summer many years ago when I applied to a number of different theatres, hoping they might ask me to join their apprentice programs and thus give me the opportunity to work in an actual professional theatre. For the purposes of turning this memory into a story, I began to imagine a "what if I had applied to the NYU workshop" scenario, and my story began to take shape in the form of the following series of events:

> I decided to apply to the NYU summer music theatre workshop.
> My parents agreed to support me if I received a scholarship.
> I worked very hard and submitted what I knew to be an excellent audition.
> I was accepted into the program, but...
> I was not awarded the scholarship I hoped for.
> Without the scholarship, I am now short $1,000 for the tuition.

I have to convince my father to pay the extra
money.
If I fail to convince him, I cannot go.

These events were the foundation of my story, and as I wrote
them down, I made them more personal and more powerful by
making certain choices. I chose to think that I had worked very
hard on the video audition and that I was proud of the results. I
provided myself with a scenario where I almost, but not quite, got
the outcome I wanted from submitting the video. I chose to be
short an amount of money that was not outlandish but still significant, and I chose my father as the person I needed to convince,
because he would be harder to convince than my mother. These
personalized and "empowered" events brought me to a place in my
story where I was faced with the very real possibility of not getting
what I wanted. These events heightened the dramatic conflict in
the scenario I was devising. They became the "building blocks" for
a dramatic circumstance that had enough power to compel me to
take action.

I now have to decide what steps to take so that the conflict will
continue to grow and reach a point of crisis. The conflict exists
between the other character in my story—my father—and me, and
we will reach a point of crisis when our conflict rises to such a level
that it absolutely must be addressed and resolved. There must be
some manner of resolution to the conflict between us, or neither
my father nor I will be able to move forward. So, I keep "writing."

My father has never been enthusiastic about my
interest in performing.
I initiate a conversation with him about the
summer program.

28

I pick a time when he is alone and a time of day
when he is normally relaxed.
I ask if he will pay the rest of the tuition.
My father tells me that my not getting the scholarship indicates to him that I'm not really
suited to be a performer.
What he says is very hurtful and makes me want
to lash out at him.

To me this is a clear point of crisis. Things couldn't get any worse. My father has essentially told me that he believes I am not really good enough to be a performer. In that moment, not only do I doubt that I can achieve my objective—the money for the workshop—but I also doubt my own sense of who I am and how I'm perceived by my father. Without even thinking about it, I know that I must find the words that will change my father's perception of me and convince him to support me in my pursuit of my dream. If I do not take action at this moment, I am certainly going to lose, and my summer-workshop story will not only be over, but it will also have a very unhappy ending.

I now, as the character in my story, want this thing so badly. I want not only the money but also my father's respect. My need is so strong and my fear of failing is so overpowering that without even thinking twice, I begin to explain to my father everything that this means to me. I communicate with a commitment and clarity that I have never had before, because the only thing I see in front of me is the thing I must achieve and the person who can help me achieve it. I know that in the words I choose and the way I say them, I must make grown-up choices. I cannot throw a tantrum or threaten to run away. If I behave that way, even though it is tempting and my gut wants to send me in that direction, I will never win my father's respect. And without his respect, I am never going to get the money.

If I act out this story, I will, by creating and then living inside this circumstance, be compelled to take an action for the sole purpose of getting my father's understanding and approval. If I succeed, my father will demonstrate his approval by paying for the summer program. I will have utilized my dramatic circumstance to place myself in a position where I know exactly what I need and why I need it. I have to find the words to say, and the best way to say them, that will change my father's mind. That becomes the reason why I will sing my song. That is, more importantly, why I will have *no choice* but to sing my song. My focus will be only on my father, because he holds the answer to my problem. My father is the only person who can give me the thing I want, and convincing him is the only way that I can achieve my goal.

In creating my story, I placed myself in a situation that resonates with my own life. Based on my own experience, it is a story that means something to me, and therefore it is a story that stimulates my imagination. I can actually see it happening. I can see it happening even though it never actually did happen, and my own father was always very supportive of the things I wanted to do and would never have suggested that I was not talented enough to do those things. My story is one that springs from "What if I had parents who never supported my dreams?" It is not something that is real, but it is something I can have fun imagining.

Approaching a Story from the Other Side

In exploring and identifying the elements of my summer-workshop story, I put myself into a situation that was designed to spur me into taking action. That action, if I were a student in one of my classes, would take the form of the song I was going to sing. Most of the time, however, performers do not create circumstances and then look for an appropriate song. Performers usually start with the song, and along with that song comes the "behavior" that the song's writers are expecting the performer to act out.

When you begin work on a song, you start with the music and lyrics on the page: the words you are going to speak and the pitches and rhythms you are going to use when you speak them. Much of what you are going to do has been prescribed by the people who wrote the song. They have determined your language, your tempo, your momentum, and your pauses. Your behavior has been laid out for you. But you know there is a lot more to it than that. You have to bring the song to life, and that requires much more insight and effort than just following a blueprint laid out for you by the people who wrote the song.

The challenge, and the fun, is to figure out how you can most effectively arrive at the behavior the writers have given you. You want to sing your songs as if those words and notes have never been sung before. You want your audience to experience each song as if you just "wrote" it, and this requires that you engage your imagination, your personality, your intelligence, and your musicianship—in a word, your talent.

In order to do that, we most often approach a song from the other direction. We start with the behavior we have been handed and then work backward to create a dramatic circumstance that will motivate that behavior. From this perspective, each song you sing must be solved as if it were a mystery and you are the detective assigned to the case. You must arrive at that behavior in such a way that the actions you take resonate truthfully with both you and your audience. You must figure out what situation and what series of events would require you to "speak" those words, make those sounds, and behave in the way the authors have described.

Let's play detective. The great Sherlock Holmes is confronted by a mystery. He arrives on the scene after the crime has been committed. The main events of the story have already taken place. Sherlock's job is to study the evidence so that he can put together a scenario that explains how everything he sees in front of him actually came to be. Once he has a scenario that explains the events in front of him, he will have no trouble identifying the person who stole the jewels, wrote the threatening letter, pulled the trigger, or put the poison in the teapot. Sherlock will be able to identify the criminal because within the scenario he created, he will be able to identify the person who had the motive to commit the crime. For our purposes, you are not looking for the criminal. You are, however, very much studying the evidence at hand in order to create a scenario that will "explain" what has happened and then motivate the song you are going to sing.

How does Sherlock put together his scenario? A criminal's motivation will always be the key to unlocking the puzzle. Therefore, Sherlock looks for the reasons why. Why would a person do these things? What would that person be hoping to accomplish by taking these actions? Sherlock looks at the "why" because he knows that the "why" will invariably lead him to the "who." You want to look at the "why" because it will lead you to the "what." Motivation is the key to behavior, and motivation will be your key to stepping into the shoes of the characters you play. When you step into those shoes, you will begin to experience that circumstance as if it were happening to you. You will experience a need that is the same as the character's, and you will derive from that need the fuel that is going to propel you toward taking action in order to get the thing you want, the thing you must have.

Putting the Dramatic into Circumstance

The story you devise that explains the situation in which you find yourself and the decisions you make in regard to what you are going to do about that situation are the source material for your dramatic circumstance. A dramatic circumstance is simply a concise articulation of the dramatic elements in a story that you have identified, explored, and refined in a way that will compel you to take an action. These elements are what you can derive from any conflict-ridden situation. The very term *dramatic circumstance* tells us that the situation itself is powerful enough—compelling enough—to rise to the level of drama. A circumstance that rises to the level of drama is one that is potent enough to require action. A dramatic circumstance must be compelling enough to make you actually do something.

Wanting to tell your girlfriend you love her just because you feel a sudden impulse to tell her would make for a perfectly "nice" situation that would lead to little in the way of dramatic behavior. It might make your girlfriend very happy, but your audience will likely be looking for more. What if your girlfriend is about to leave for college and you are afraid you might lose her, and so you have decided that before she goes you are going to ask her to marry you? That's the stuff of a dramatic circumstance!

The Building Blocks

Each dramatic circumstance you set out to create will be constructed from four essential components. The first is the series of events that place you in your current situation. Those events must bring you to a point of crisis, and from within that moment of crisis, you will readily be able to identify your *problem*, your *other*, and your *objective*. The laying out of your events and the naming of your problem, other, and objective are the steps you must take every time you analyze a song, and they are the steps you must take for every song you sing.

Let's look again at our summer workshop story. My situation began with my decision that I wanted to go—that I *had* to go—to the workshop. The subsequent events brought me to the moment in which my father suggested that my not getting the scholarship was an indication that I really did not have what it would take to be a successful singer and actor. My father was essentially telling me that I was not good enough. That was my point of crisis.

Why is that a point of crisis? Because I knew at that moment that my father was wrong and something had to be done. It had to be done right that very minute or I would lose the thing that I wanted so desperately. At that point, nothing could stop me from taking action. Because I had reached a point of crisis, I was able to instinctively make my strongest, clearest choices for my problem, my other, and my objective. From your perspective of someone caught at a point of real crisis, you need to ask yourself the following questions:

- What is the thing that is wrong that must be fixed?
- Who is the person I believe can fix it?
- What must I get that person to do in order to fix the thing that is wrong?

The thing that is wrong is that I feel hurt and humiliated because my father thinks so little of my ability, and I am afraid that he is never going to support me and my dream of being a performer. That is my *problem*.

My *other*, the person who can fix the thing that is wrong, is clearly my father, because he has the ability to believe in me and support me.

I have to find a way to get my father to see me in a different light, to understand and respect the depth of my passion and commitment so that he will then agree to pay the full tuition for the summer program. That is my *objective*.

Other and *objective* are the absolute keys to a successful performance. If you have no time to do any other work in preparation for performance, I suggest that you make a strong decision about who are you singing to and what you want that person to do.

Providing yourself with an *other* and an *objective* is the ultimate goal of the dramatic circumstance process. What makes this process so valuable to a performer is that your other and your objective will inspire you to take a clear action, and they will fuel that action throughout the time that you are taking it. This way of thinking about your work makes your objective—that thing you must achieve come hell or high water—come to life. In addition, a fully committed pursuit of your objective is the most effective, efficient, and powerful method by which you can get your instrument to function in the way you need it to function.

As I have already said, it is impossible in a book for you to see for yourself the impact this process can have on someone's performance. So let me share with you what one singer recently reported in a written response to a coaching.

> I struggled to come up with a circumstance for the song. The first time I sang through it I was trying to put myself in a vulnerable state and feel the general concept of loneliness, which is definitely not the easiest and most effective way to communicate anything. I think that I was breathing well

this first time, which is at least something helpful. After we discussed my circumstance I realized that my situation left out the specific details—the time, exact location, person I'm with, etc.—which are the most important parts of the situation. I had intentionally left the situation very vague because I was trying to keep it in line with what I thought was the show's circumstance. You then brought up the idea of crisis, which is the greatest point of conflict. The crisis in the new circumstance for this song was that this girl was about to leave me, and if I allowed that to happen I would have lost her without ever having said anything. With the crisis designated, it is very easy to pick out the problem and objective and other. It is interesting to think about, because the crisis always exists within a circumstance, but when you actually take the time to specify exactly what it is, the other pieces fall into place much more easily. We then talked about how my objective was to get her phone number, and how the objective should always be something positive. I should try to obtain something rather than try to prevent something like, in this case, trying to stop her from leaving. That gave me something physical to attempt to achieve and added clarity to the circumstance.

Seaman Knapp was proved right yet again. The student "got it" once he actually "did it."

4

Creating Your Dramatic Circumstance

W hen working with music theatre or opera material, your situation will most often come out of the plot of the play itself, but plot by itself will never give you a reason to act, and a story is not going to be of any value to you until you make it your own. In order to bring a character or a song to life—and that is what you are always trying to do—that character's story and song must become *your* story and *your* song.

At the center of any good story is a person with a problem. In the songs you sing and the roles you play, you must become that person with the problem. If you have a big enough problem, one that is sufficiently *problematic*, you will have no choice but to do something about it. The thing to keep in mind is that the bigger the problem, the "bigger" the behavior that will grow out of that problem. For our first coaching, we are going to follow the steps that one actor took in order to apply the dramatic circumstance process to a specific song from a specific show.

Katerina is coaching "Where Is Love?" from Lionel Bart's musical play *Oliver!*, which is based on the Charles Dickens novel *Oliver Twist*. Even though the character of Oliver is a boy, the role is often played by a girl, and "Where Is Love?" is a song that is easily, and often, sung out of the context of the show.

WW: Katerina, tell me about the situation you are in.

K: I'm an orphan named Oliver, and I've been living in a workhouse. But now I...er...I forgot the name of the character. I think it's Mr. Bumble. He's sold me to the Sowerberrys.

WW: Okay. Everything you are saying is true, but let's not confuse situation or dramatic circumstance with plot. Plot will help you articulate a specific situation, but in order to create your dramatic circumstance, you must tell the story. You have to lay out a series of events that are going to lead you to your point of crisis.

K: And that's when I'll sing.

WW: Exactly.

Plot is always helpful as a source for information and ideas, but without you telling the story in your own terms, plot is not going to provide you either a situation in which to imagine yourself or a dramatic circumstance that is going to inspire you to take action. That being said, it is almost always the case that the writers of a successful play have created a powerful story from which you can extract a lot of the information you need. Since it is Katerina's job to devise a story with herself as the central character, and since Oliver is a part that Katerina could conceivably play, in this example it does make sense for her to utilize plot elements of the script itself. However, Katerina does not actually have to know a thing about the Dickens novel, or Lionel Bart's script, in order to create a circumstance that will inspire an action that begins with her asking the question "Where is love?" This would be true if she were singing the song by itself, and it would also be true if she were playing the role of Oliver in a production of the show.

WW: Your task is to create and explore dramatic elements for your own circumstance. The elements that you create yourself are the ones that will have the greatest impact on your work. So let us lay out the elements of your situation. What are the events that lead up to the point where you sing the first words of your song?

K: Okay. Oliver is an orphan who lives with lots of other boys in a workhouse.

WW: That is a good first statement. But from here on out, I want you to talk in the first person. "I" am an orphan, and "I" live with a lot of other boys in a workhouse.

K: Got it.

WW: And why do I want you to do that?

K: Because it helps me imagine that I am actually in the situation?

WW: You got it. Start again.

K: I am an orphan who lives in a workhouse with lots of other little boys.

WW: When did you become an orphan?

K: Well, my father was never a part of the picture, and I think my mother died when I was born.

WW: So how might that change your first statement?

K: I am an orphan, and I never knew my mother or father.

WW: Better, right? An orphan who has never known any parent at all is going to be a different person than one whose parents might have died when he was older. Is he going to be better off or worse?

K: For me it would be worse never to have known my parents.

WW: Why?

K: Because I've never had anyone who loved me.

WW: And that sparks your imagination in a more specific way, which will give you more ideas to work with.

K: It makes the situation more painful.

WW: Good. Let's find some more pain. What's it like in the workhouse?

K: Crowded, cold, not enough to eat.

WW: So give me the first two sentences again.

K: I am an orphan who has never known a father or mother, and I live in terrible conditions in a cold, crowded workhouse.

WW: Why are those sentences better?

K: Because they mean more. They are more... alive.

WW: Keep going.

K: I am a troublemaker.

WW: Why?

K: Because I speak up and ask for more food, and that starts a riot.

WW: Then what happens?

K: The man who runs the workhouse sells me to an undertaker.

WW: And then what happens?

K: I get into trouble again.

WW: How?

K: The other boy that works there says bad things about my mother, and I start a fight with him. So they lock me up alone in a room full of coffins. And they leave me with nothing to eat or drink.

WW: And that's when you sing this song.

K: Right.

WW: Good. Nice work. You now have a well-articulated series of events. And keep in mind that you can always go back and revise those events as you find words and images that are more powerful for you.

Let's take a look at the "list" of events Katerina made in her dramatic circumstance that are going to lead her to a point of crisis. This list is something that Katerina can continue to explore and revise, and these events will form the basis for the story that she is going to tell herself every time she works on this song. It can be very helpful to take the time to put the list on paper.

I am an orphan who has never known my father or mother.

I live in a cold, crowded workhouse where there is never enough to eat.

I ask for more food and inadvertently start a riot.

The owner of the workhouse sells me to an undertaker.

The other boy who works there says terrible
things about my mother.

I start a fight with him, which escalates into
another riot.

They lock me up alone in a room full of coffins
with no food or water.

WW: So, we have a situation. Has that situation
brought you to a point of crisis?

K: I think so.

WW: And that point of crisis is...?

K: My life is intolerable. I would rather die than
continue the way it is.

WW: That sounds like a crisis to me. So out of those
circumstances, how would you describe your
problem?

K: I'm locked up.

WW: Why is that a problem?

K: Isn't it obvious?

WW: Not to me. Maybe you're just relieved to have
some time on your own.

K: But I'm in prison.

WW: Then say that.

K: I'm imprisoned. Against my will.

WW: And you feel...?

K: Trapped.

WW: Good. "Trapped" sounds like a problem.

K: Caught in a cage.

WW: Even better.

K: I don't have any food or water.

WW: Maybe you're not hungry or thirsty.

K: Okay. I see where this is going. I'm hungry and
       thirsty. I'm cold...alone.

WW: Okay. Can you take the idea of "alone" any
       further?

K: Well, I'm lonely. I don't have anyone who loves
       me.

WW: And how do you know that?

K: From the lyrics.

WW: What do the lyrics tell you?

K: That I'm asking where love is because I don't
       have anyone in my life who loves me.

WW: So you are lonely and unloved. Is that more
       specific than alone?

K: Much more specific.

WW: And much more useful to you as an actor.

K: The words are more powerful. They mean
       more to me.

WW: Exactly! You are lonely, unloved, cold, and
       hungry. These are problems we all understand.
       These are things we have all experienced. Per-
       haps not all at the same time, but these are
       problems with which we can identify.

K: And don't forget trapped.

WW: Lonely, unloved, cold, hungry, *and* trapped. All
       good problem stuff.

You can see how Katerina's story brings her to a point of crisis,
and out of that crisis she must identify the problem state in which
she finds herself. Katerina articulates that state with very precise
language when she says, "I am lonely, unloved, cold, hungry, and
trapped."

The words that Katerina has chosen for herself are very powerful. They are powerful words to anyone who hears them, but they have the most value in the work she is doing because they are powerful to Katerina. Anyone who is planting the words *lonely, unloved, cold, hungry,* and *trapped* into her consciousness—and who has selected those words based on what resonates with her and her own experience of those words—is going to begin to understand and experience the size of the problem in which this person finds herself. And the best part about acting is that you do not have to have been orphaned, starved, or imprisoned in order for these words to mean something to you. With whatever life experience you have had thus far, you are more than capable of imagining what it would feel like to be in this kind of situation.

You must always look for powerful language as you go about your work. The words you choose and the language to which you commit yourself can make all the difference in the world. It is through language that you organize your thoughts, and it is through the specific vocabulary you use to articulate your situation and your circumstance that you make those thoughts powerful enough to stimulate your imagination. It is through your imagination that you will most effectively engage your brain, your body, and your voice, and it is through your imagination that you will feel compelled to take action. Most importantly, the actions you take will be focused on, and fueled by, what you need to accomplish as the character you are portraying, instead of what you are hoping you might accomplish as the performer who wants to do a good job performing.

> WW: So, Kat. Now that you have articulated and imagined this particular set of problems, you need to do something about them. Right?
>
> K: Right.

WW: What are you going to do?

K: Well, I need to solve these problems. To make them go away.

WW: And how are you going to do that?

K: I have no idea.

WW: Why not?

K: Because I'm a helpless little kid.

WW: Ah, but you are a kid with a dream and a huge heart and a pure soul.

K: When you say it like that, he sounds powerful.

WW: That's the idea. Can you define the term *action* for me?

K: Sure. An action is what you do in order to get the thing you want.

WW: Perfect. And in this case your action is going to be what?

K: Whatever I do to make my problems go away.

WW: And what might that be? You are a small child being mistreated by a bunch of adults. You're locked behind closed doors. They refuse to give you food or drink. Things are looking pretty grim. What do you need?

K: A savior?

WW: You got it! You need someone who can save you.

K: But who, realistically, is that going to be?

WW: It doesn't have to be realistic. It just has to be what you want. The most powerful dramatic circumstances grow out of situations that appear hopeless. Who might, in your wildest dreams, come save you from the situation you are in?

K: Batman?

WW: Wrong era, but nice try.

K: My mother. If she were still alive.

WW: Or even if she's not. You are not making a phone call to 911. You are envisioning a scenario in which someone cares enough about you to come save you.

In every story you tell, you will be trying to get something from a person you believe has the power to solve your problem. The thing that you want is your objective, and the person from whom you are trying to get that thing is your other.

Katerina has now articulated her problem and her objective. She needs to get someone to save her, and she has identified at least one strong choice for who that person might be.

WW: So, you are going to sing to your mother.

K: Yes.

WW: Your actual mother?

K: No. The idea of a mother. Not my real mother but...like her.

WW: And what makes someone motherlike?

K: Nurturing, patient, gentle, kind.

WW: And you understand those things because of your own mother.

K: Absolutely.

WW: And you're going to envision an other who has those qualities.

K: Just like Oliver probably envisions his own mother.

WW: Good point. Is the mother you are singing to there in the room with you?

K: What do you mean? She's imaginary.

WW: Right. And that means that in your imagination
      you can put her anywhere you want her to be.
      Do you imagine her standing across the room
      looking at you?

K: Er...yes? No? I'm not sure.

WW: It's okay to be unsure. This isn't a test, and there's
      not a right answer. We're looking for ideas that
      make sense to you and then figuring out what
      impact those ideas have on your story. If your
      mother is in the room with you, and you are
      asking her, "Where is love?" what does that tell
      you?

K: That she's not a very good mother.

WW: Why is that?

K: Because if she were a good mother, I wouldn't
      have to ask.

WW: Exactly.

K: So, she's not there.

WW: Where is she?

K: In the story?

WW: In *your* story.

K: I have no idea where she is.

WW: Great. That'll work. So tell me, who are you
      singing to?

K: I am singing to my dead mother, and I have no
      idea where she is.

Katerina started by imagining that she was singing to her mother,
and then by applying a little basic psychology, she determined that
the mother she was going to envision was not in the room with her.

She provided herself an other from whom she is separated. In fact, she realized that her most potent choice was to have no idea where her mother was, in her imagination or otherwise. She encapsulated her other by saying, "I am singing to my dead mother, and I have no idea where she is."

WW: Now we need our objective. What do you want your mother to do?

K: To understand how I feel.

WW: Okay. Let's say she understands. What mother wouldn't understand? Does that solve your problem?

K: No...?

WW: Correct. Why doesn't it solve your problem?

K: Because I'm still locked up, cold, hungry, etcetera.

WW: Right. So if you can get her to understand, what might she do then?

K: Come get me?

WW: Good.

K: But that's not possible.

WW: Why not?

K: Because she's dead!

WW: Don't you ever wish for things that are impossible?

K: All the time.

WW: Then why not do that now? Try to get something that is impossible. Look for a miracle. Does that sound like dramatic behavior?

K: Sure.

WW: It's powerful stuff. And something we all actually do understand.

K: "When you wish upon a star," right?

WW: That's it. So what do you want your mother to do?

K: Appear. Come into the room.

WW: And once she's there?

K: Rescue me.

WW: Great word! *Rescue*. You need your mother to rescue you. You are alone and cold and hungry, and you want your mother to come do something about it. Is this something you can now do? Something you can act?

K: I think so. And if I think of my own mother— as if I were singing this to my own mother—it makes it even more powerful.

WW: Good. Now you're ready to occupy the circumstance that you've created.

K: But I have a question. Am I singing this as Oliver or as me?

WW: Does it matter?

K: Well, aren't we supposed to know all about the character and the story and the history? Where does that stuff figure in?

WW: Well, in my opinion Charles Dickens and Lionel Bart have already taken care of that stuff. You need to take actions in a situation using the language that was provided for you. That language is the author's responsibility, and in this case I think both Charlie and Lionel have done a pretty good job. Your job is to speak that language as if you were in that circumstance. The audience will then fill in the blanks.

K: What do you mean by "speak the language"?

WW: I mean that you must be able to occupy a story as if the language of that story were your own. The story's cadence, vocabulary, and inflection must be your own.

K: But you're saying that the character doesn't really matter?

WW: This character only exists when you give him a voice. What matters is the extent to which you are able to successfully occupy the circumstance that you've created in order to speak and sing the words provided to you by the author.

There are those who certainly do not share my view of character and an actor's obligation to character. I find that people in music theatre are particularly uncomfortable with taking away the standard "assignments" that young actors are meant to follow in search for the "character" they are going to play. I am going to look at the subject of character in much more detail in chapter 10, "Freeing Yourself from Obligation." For the moment, I will leave you with one of my favorite quotes from David Mamet's book *True and False: Heresy and Common Sense for the Actor* (Vintage Books, 1999), a book I highly recommend that all actors read, in spite of the fact that some acting teachers I know highly recommend they *not* read it.

> There is no character. There are only lines upon a page. They are lines of dialogue meant to be said by the actor. When he or she says them simply, in an attempt to achieve an object more or less like that suggested by the author, the audience sees an illusion of a character upon the stage.

Moving Right Along

I would like to repeat something important I said in chapter 3:

> The laying out of your events and the naming of your
> problem, other, and objective are the steps you must take
> every time you analyze a song, and they are the steps you
> must take for every song you sing.

You saw in the steps Katerina took in her coaching how she was able to tell her story. She explored and articulated her dramatic circumstance, and she is now ready to utilize that circumstance to find the impulse, the motivation, she needs to sing the song.

How will she do that? She will occupy the dramatic circumstance she has created. That is what we are going to do in the next chapter.

5

Occupying
Your Dramatic
Circumstance

At the end of my first year at the American Academy of Dramatic Arts, the guest speaker at the senior graduation was Helen Hayes, considered by many at that time to be the "First Lady of the American Theatre." Miss Hayes had an acting career that spanned almost seventy years and is one of only eleven people in history to have been awarded an Emmy, a Grammy, a Tony, and an Oscar. She told us she believed an actor was someone who could look offstage at a brick wall and see a rose garden. Given my training and experience up to that point, I thought she meant that an actor could look at a brick wall and imagine seeing a rose garden, or could appear to be seeing a rose garden. It took many years of acting, directing, and teaching for me to finally realize that Miss Hayes meant exactly what she said, and that was: "An actor can look offstage at a brick wall and see a rose garden." She was talking about the power of suggestion and our ability to make use of our innate suggestibility.

We love to get caught up in a story. It is actually something we do, and something we have done to us, all the time. Look what happens when we go to the movies. The size of the picture, the volume of sound, and the compelling nature of the story take command of our senses and pull us into a world in which we suddenly believe in those pictures on the screen as if those events were actually happening—even as if they were actually happening to us. When your hero is walking down a long, dark corridor, knowing full well that the villain is lurking in the darkness ready to pounce at any moment, you walk down that corridor right along with him. Or perhaps I should say, you can if you choose to. Actors are the kind of people, as I talked about earlier, who *choose* to step into the stories they tell. They are not content to sit on the outside and watch their stories go by. And that is what Helen Hayes was talking about.

The suggestive power of movies themselves, along with the fact that moviegoing is an experience to which we can all relate, is why I like to talk about this process as if you are using your imagination to make a movie in your head in which you are playing the starring role. Once you can see your dramatic circumstance happening right in front of you on a screen thirty feet high and sixty feet wide, you will more easily be able to step into that circumstance.

Creating a dramatic circumstance is your first step. Occupying that circumstance is your next step—the crucial step. In fact, occupying the circumstances that you create is the most important part of this process. It is the key to a successful performance. In the previous chapter, we saw Katerina lay out the events of the story that bring her character, Oliver, to the crisis situation that compels him to sing "Where Is Love?" Katerina then utilized her imagination to place herself in that situation. Utilizing "what if," she was able to create the dramatic circumstance that she needed to propel her into the song, and she created that circumstance by identifying its three fundamental components:

- Her resonantly articulated and personal problem
- Her clearly envisioned other
- Her compelling objective

Katerina articulated these components in a vocabulary that resonated with her own life experience, and all three came together to form her own particular, personal dramatic circumstance. She is now ready to put that circumstance to work, and she is going to do that by taking specific steps that will allow her to occupy the circumstance that she has created.

What does it mean to occupy a circumstance? The dramatic elements that you have created are the "seeds" for the actions you are going to take. Occupying your circumstance is the process whereby you take those "seeds" and "plant" them into your consciousness.

And how do you do that? You begin by taking yourself through a three-step physical process called *centering*. The centering process, and its impact on a performer's work, is so physical, individual, and personal that it is difficult to describe in a book. I have provided a detailed description of the process in chapter 8, "Supplying the Fuel," along with step-by-step instructions on how to take yourself through each of the centering phases. For now I want you to observe how Katerina follows my instructions to center herself so that she can more fully step inside the story she created. As we go through this part of the coaching, I suggest that you follow the instructions I give Katerina by breathing whenever I ask—or remind—Katerina to do so. You can easily do that as you are reading, and it will help you take in the experience in a more immediate way, as if you were actually in the room or as if you were the person being coached.

Stepping Inside the Story

At the end of the previous chapter, we left Katerina ready to sing "Where Is Love?" She had articulated her problem as being "alone, cold, hungry, and locked up." She then determined that her mother was the strongest choice that she could make for her other, and she articulated her objective as needing to be rescued.

WW: What does "rescue" look like?

K: I...I have no idea.

WW: Actually, you do. *Rescue* is your word, and it came from your consciousness, and in your consciousness there is a movie of what "rescue" looks like and feels like.

K: Okay.

WW: So. I want you to shake out and take a couple of really big breaths. You're going to stand up straight. Release your jaw. Inhale gently and evenly, and then release your breath with the same gentle, even flow of air. Inhale on a count of four, and exhale on a count of six.

The goal here is to establish an even flow of air. The released jaw, gently letting go right at the point in front of your ears where your jaw hinges, will facilitate the ease of the airflow.

WW: Keep in mind that you are not pushing the jaw down. You are not trying to drop it. It is just an easy, gentle release that leaves your face feeling relaxed. Your jaw hangs loosely. Your mouth is slightly open. There should be a small space between your upper and lower teeth—no more than the width of your little fingertip.

K: Okay.

WW: Focus on a spot in front of you. Think that you are pulling your breath from that spot and then sending your breath energy back to that same point of focus.

K: Okay.

WW: And as we continue, I want you to focus only on your breathing and your point of focus. You are going to listen to what I'm saying, but you don't need to acknowledge that you've heard me. Let the words that I'm speaking just sink into your consciousness. If I ask a question, or ask you to repeat any words that I'm saying, just do so simply and clearly so that you don't lose your focus or interrupt your measured breath. Now . . . say, "I'm cold."

K: I'm cold.

WW: Think about what that means. Can you feel the sensation of cold in your hands? In your feet? Can you feel cold come into your body as you take each breath?

Katerina nods slightly.

WW: See the room around you. What's there?

K: It's dark. There are lots of shadows. There are things moving in the shadows.

WW: What kind of things?

K: Things that would hurt me.

WW: Keep going.

K: I'm hungry.

WW: What does that feel like?

K: It's a pain. My stomach hurts.

WW: Okay. Keep breathing.

K: I'm alone.

WW: Yes…?

K: I am alone and going to be lonely for the rest of my life.

WW: Now put all of that together.

K: I am locked up in a cold and empty room. I'm hungry. It's dark. I'm alone, and I'm afraid I am going to be lonely for the rest of my life.

WW: Keep breathing, and tell me, from that place that you just described, what you see in front of you.

K: I don't see anything. Just the darkness. And the shadows.

WW: Can you imagine your mother?

K: Yes. Barely. She's in the distance, very far away.

WW: What is she doing?

K: She's looking for me.

WW: Let her find you. See her seeing you.

K: She's smiling!

WW: Keep going.

K: She's moving closer and holding out her arms.

WW: Let her find you.

K: She comes up to me and wraps her arms around me.

WW: And…?

K: I don't feel cold any more.

WW: Anything else?

K: She tells me that everything is going to be okay.

WW: Good. That's excellent work! Now shake out a bit. Continue to let your breath move freely. Nice deep breaths as you come back into the room.

Katerina takes a minute to shake out and breathe.

WW: How was that?

K: Interesting.

WW: It was. Very interesting. Do you have information you didn't have before?

K: Absolutely.

WW: What's different?

K: Well, it's like the things that I had made part of my circumstance are all still there, but they are in a different part of me.

WW: What things?

K: My story. My problem. All of it.

WW: Where are they?

K: They're in my body, not just in my head.

WW: And how does that feel?

K: It feels great.

WW: And...?

K: I know what I need to do.

WW: Which is?

K: I need to get my mother to appear. To smile at me. To take me in her arms and tell me that everything is going to be all right.

WW: But you knew that before.

K: It's different now. It's inside me. It's not just a
       thought. My whole...being...all of me knows
       what I need, and it makes me want to get it.
WW: Terrific. It sounds as if you are ready to sing
       your song.

Katerina organized her breath and her thoughts and then utilized the resulting heightened state of awareness to envision her
circumstance as if she were in a movie. She was able to actually
"see" her problem and her other, and most importantly, she was
able to envision exactly what she wanted her other to do. By connecting her description of her problem state to a low and centered
breath, Katerina was able to put herself in position to participate in
the movie she was creating. She utilized her breath and her thoughts
to occupy her circumstance. The words you choose become the
instructions that you give to yourself. The way you breathe allows
those instructions to move deeper into your consciousness. It is
that combination of words and breath that will allow your mind to
begin to "see" the thing that you are imagining.

The dramatic potential of Katerina's circumstance lies in the fact
that it is personal and specific to her own experience and her own
perspective on life. You can see why clear and potent language plays
such a pivotal role in the work we are doing. You must incorporate
a language—a vocabulary specific to you—that will resonate in
your center, not just in your head. The time Katerina spent centering will allow her to connect to those personal elements that will
provide the most potent fuel with which she will be able to sing
her song. Whether Katerina is singing "Where Is Love?" in the
practice room, a voice lesson, a class, an audition, or a performance, she will be able to bring both herself and her song to life
by occupying the circumstance she has created. Whenever and

wherever she wants, she can occupy her circumstance by retracing the same steps she took in her coaching. These are the steps that will take her down the path of someone who feels unloved and alone. This is how she will walk in the shoes of someone who wants more than anything in the world for her mother to come rescue her.

This is also how Katerina will be able to focus totally on the work she has to do as the character singing the song and not let herself be distracted by all of the things that so often distract singers while they are trying to do their work. This ability to let the rest of the world slip into the background while you just carry out the task in front of you is what makes this work so empowering and so liberating.

In for a Penny…

For the purpose of illustrating how you occupy a dramatic circumstance, let me just say for now that you implement the centering process in order to transport yourself into the dramatic circumstance you have devised.

What do I mean by "transport"? I mean that the physical elements in the literal space you occupy begin to fade into the background. In addition—and more importantly—the parts of you that want to watch what you are doing and judge how well you are doing, and thereby distract you from the more important tasks at hand, also fade into the background. As these distracting elements fade away, you will find that the only things that exist for you are your other and the thing that you want and need him or her to do. You use your breath and your mind to envision a different world than the one you literally occupy. This allows you to experience a circumstance as if the elements of that circumstance were actually happening to you at that very moment.

Another way of describing the steps you take while centering is that you talk yourself into believing in the circumstance that you have created. One might even describe the process as a kind of self-hypnosis. Hypnosis is the induction of a state of consciousness in which a person becomes highly responsive to suggestion or direction. In the centering process, you are the one doing the inducing—hence, self-hypnosis.

And what is it you "suggest" or "direct"? You can suggest almost anything you want and direct your consciousness to almost anywhere. It's how you arrive at the "believe" part of make-believe.

The occupying of a dramatic circumstance is a learned skill. If you practice it diligently and daily, it will get better and better, and there is absolutely no question that it is fun to do, even when the circumstances you are choosing to occupy are not. I believe that transporting yourself into a level of consciousness deeper in your imagination and lower in your body is the phase of the centering process that is most critical to your success. It is something that is amazing to watch as an actor moves successfully into this phase of the work. In chapter 14, "Playing the Brain Game," I am going to discuss the scientific hypothesis of brain evolution and neural function that I think supports this work and helps explain why it is so effective.

Truth to Tell

My belief in the dramatic circumstance process and my commitment to it as a powerful working method for actors and singers are the result of the years I have spent seeing the work my students do when they follow these steps. When they think and breathe and take the time they need, the changes in their work are immediate, and they are profound. Every day I get to see singers experience a new kind of freedom and clarity that is as exciting for me as it is for them.

It has been my experience that artists of all disciplines seek, in the pursuit of their art, two fundamental experiences: freedom and truth.

What is freedom? Freedom is the sensation of having liberated yourself from the limitations of self-consciousness that can constrict you as you study, practice, rehearse, and perform. Ultimate freedom is freedom from fear. Everything else will follow.

What is truth? Truth is allowing yourself to see, with unadorned clarity, what you know about yourself and what you have learned in the course of your life about human behavior, and then—and this is the key—having the courage to take action based on that knowledge.

The actors and singers I work with certainly want above all for their work to be honest, and I am sure you are no different. You are absolutely committed to achieving vocal and dramatic freedom, but at the same time you want that freedom to come from a place you believe in. But all too often it is because you do not "believe" that you will not act. Your desire for honesty causes you to question every natural impulse, and you become mired in a veritable no-man's-land between what you want and what you fear.

This commitment to honesty is often articulated as a desire to be "real." You have probably expressed that desire yourself. While I absolutely understand what you mean by the word *real*, I am going to begin our work together by asking you to incorporate what I think will be a significant change in vocabulary. I want you to set aside the word *real* and replace it with *true*. What you want—what all singers, actors, directors, writers, and artists want—is for your work to be true.

What is the difference between real and true? As the curtain falls at the end of *West Side Story*, Tony is dead, and Maria is left to pick up the pieces of her life. That is what has happened to the characters in the story, but it is not real. No one, unless something has gone terribly wrong in that particular performance of *West Side Story*, has died. However, if the singer playing Maria has committed to a process whereby she has chosen to behave truthfully, she will have taken some time, in the course of that process, to imagine what it would be like to lose someone she loves. Not—and this is very important—to imagine what that loss would feel like in an emotional sense, but to imagine what that loss would feel like in one's body, at the very center of one's being. The question I would ask the actress, and the question I would want her to ask herself, is "What do you do when life slugs you in the gut?"

If our truth-seeking Maria has imagined the emptiness, the pain, and the disorientation that would surely follow the loss of someone you dearly love and with whom you were planning to spend the rest of your life, she will be ready to take on the death of the lover she has placed at the center of her story. And note that the vocabulary here—*emptiness, pain, disorientation*—is that of actual physical sensations, not emotional states.

Maria sees Tony slipping away from her, and she wants only one thing—the exact same thing anyone would want who is in those circumstances—to keep her loved one alive. And when the actress tries with all of her might to keep Tony alive, she is going to fail, because that is what the writer has determined. And as she fails, she will experience a true sense of loss. When the actress playing Maria has that experience, the tragedy of that loss will resonate with every person who is fortunate enough to be present for that moment. That includes the other actors, the crew in the wings, the musicians in the pit, and—lest we forget the most important people of all—the members of the audience who came to the theatre because they wanted to share in that moment of truth.

Always remember: in the theatre nothing is real, but anything can be true. In the stories we tell, we create illusions of reality, and when fully realized, those stories and the illusions they help us create resonate with real power, because they strike chords of what is true.

Freedom and truth are what, I believe, all artists seek every single day. We look for that, whether it be consciously or unconsciously, every time we do our work. Freedom and truth are intrinsically linked. The one begets the other. I believe that it is through your pursuit of and commitment to freedom and truth that you can become truly empowered as an artist, and empowerment is the state for which the artist constantly strives.

6

Meet the "Committee"

Y ou know what they say about the camel: it is a horse that was
designed by a committee. I think that everyone can appreciate
both the humor and the truth in that statement, and anyone who
has ever worked at a university can appreciate the humor while still
feeling the despair. The dictionary tells us that a committee is "a
body of persons delegated to consider, investigate, take action on,
or report on some matter." For our purposes, you are the "matter"
on which the committee is focusing its attention, and the committee
is made up of anyone who has managed to get inside your head
and issue reports as to what is going well—or, as is more often the
case, what is not going so well.

Charlotte—a graduate of the Steinhardt School's Master of Music
Program in Music Theatre Performance—came to the program a
talented, intelligent, and hard-working singer with quite a bit of
performance experience. She got up in class to work one day, and
shortly after she started singing, she suddenly stopped.

WW:	Why did you stop?
C:	It was the committee.

WW: The committee?

C: That's what I call them.

WW: That's what you call who?

C: The voices in my head that keep me from doing my work.

WW: The voices in your head?

C: The voices of all the people who watch me all the time and tell me if I do something wrong.

WW: Or even if you *might* do something wrong?

C: That's them. That's the committee.

WW: So...we're talking an actual psychotic episode.

C: No! We're just talking about everyday performer anxiety and neuroses.

WW: And this committee can get pretty noisy?

C: Very noisy...and very insistent.

WW: Describe what happens.

C: Okay. I get up. I'm ready to work. I've done my homework and my preparation. I know what steps I'm going to take and what I need to do. Then, just as I'm ready to sing, the "committee" inside my head starts talking. My "you haven't really done your work" voice tells me that I'm not actually prepared, or that I'm not warmed up, or that I don't know my words. My "you can't sing" voice tells me that I'm going to have trouble with the high notes at the end of the song. My "you can't act" voice tells me that all the choices I've made are all wrong.

Other students in the class jumped in.

St#1:   The "fashion police" tell me that I've worn the wrong dress.

St#2:   The "music police" tell me that I've chosen the wrong song.

WW: How many of you change your song at the very last minute, right as your name is called?

St#3:   I do that all the time! I invariably feel less secure once I start singing.

WW: What else?

St#4:   The "talent police" tell me that I'm never going to make it in this business anyway and that I'm a fool to keep putting myself in this situation.

WW: So the committee, made up of all these "policemen," just takes over. At the very least, they distract you. At worst, they actually bring your work to a halt.

C: Like they did today. They got so loud that I lost track of everything I set out to do. I just get lost, and it feels terrible.

WW: Have you ever actually stopped at an audition?

C: No. Thank God!

WW: Why not?

C: Well, at an audition you know that you just have to keep going. Even though it feels really crummy, and you know it's not the kind of work you really can do.

WW: Why did you stop here in class?

C: Because I could. Because I didn't want to just keep going and end up feeling bad about the time I spent working.

WW: Good for you. You decided, as part of your work process, to actually talk about the thing that keeps you from doing your work.

C: I thought I just stopped.

WW: You did. But isn't it obvious that we have a teachable moment here? You're talking about something that everyone in the room understands. Something that everyone goes through. Or has certainly gone through. It's important.

Have you had similar experiences? Does your own "committee" store up ammunition so that it can unleash a barrage of criticism so distracting that you find yourself unable to think? Unable to breathe? Unable to access the things that you have been working so hard to do—the things that you absolutely know you know how to do?

It was brave of Charlotte to talk about the things that were getting in her way, and it was generous of her to share this experience with the class. She described something with which everyone in the room could clearly identify, including me, and we discovered that talking about the things that frighten us can sometimes make them less scary. We so often think that it is our job to soldier on through whatever is distracting or frightening or debilitating. I think that the first step—the most significant step—we can take in addressing the things that get in the way of our work is to acknowledge that these things do exist and that they can be very powerful.

But doesn't that just make them more powerful? In fact, it doesn't. Nothing is more powerful than an internal voice, particularly a judgmental and insistent voice that you try to ignore or suppress.

So how do you silence that voice? You don't. You find something to focus on that is more powerful. You find something louder. You make your "movie" as compelling as possible and occupy your dramatic circumstance as fully as possible. You take the same steps that Katerina took. You center, breathe, and focus on what is happening to you.

Does that "fix" the problem? The extent to which anyone can make her or his committee of critics go away, or even quiet down for a little while, is different for each individual. Based on my own life experience, I would say that your personal "committee" is something that you will have to deal with, at least to some degree, throughout your life and your career. It is also something that you must ultimately deal with in your own way. I have found, however, that the dramatic circumstance process works for everyone who gives it a try.

Your job—your I'm-getting-up-to-sing-now-and-don't-want-to-be-derailed-by-outside-forces job—is to replace those distracting voices with a single, more powerful voice. You replace them with a voice that is telling you what you have to do and that the thing you have to do is so important you must give it your undivided attention. When you get distracted, you ask yourself, "What is my problem? Who is my other? What do I want my other to do?"

WW: The committee doesn't win every time you get up to sing, does it?

C: No. It doesn't.

WW: I've seen you do really powerful work. What accounts for that?

C: If I know just what I need to do.

WW: And...?

C: If the need to do it is strong enough.

WW: So what does that tell you?

C: That I need to take enough time when I center to get myself to the place where I have to take an action.

WW: And what happens then?

C: The thing I need to do becomes more important than the voices that are telling me I can't do it.

WW: Right. Powerful work is neither an accident nor luck. Powerful work is a choice you make. It is the result of the way you think and the steps you follow.

The song Charlotte was working on, "I've Never Said I Love You" from the Jerry Herman musical *Dear World* (based on Jean Giraudoux's poetic satire *The Madwoman of Chaillot*), is one in which a young woman declares that she is not going to say the words "I love you" until the right man—the man to whom she wants to say those words—comes along. Charlotte had devised a circumstance in which she was a young woman who believed, in spite of a number of unhappy relationships, that the right man was somewhere out there in the world and worth waiting for. Her other was a woman she worked for, an older and much more cynical person who wanted Charlotte to give up any silly notions she might have about meeting the right guy and living happily ever after.

WW: What do you need your boss to do?

C: I need her to shut up.

WW: You don't want to hear anything she has to say.

C: Right.

WW: So why don't you leave?

C: What?

WW: If you just leave you don't have to listen to her.

C: But I have to—

WW: Have to what?

C: Er...sing the song?

WW: But your character isn't singing a song. Your character is simply trying to sort out her feelings in relation to her complicated romantic history, and while she's trying to do that, her boss is giving her a hard time.

C: Okay. Then I want her to shut up.

WW: And that's it?

C: Well, if she shuts up I won't have to listen to her.

WW: And do the lyrics of the song say, "Shut up, you hateful old woman"?

C: No.

WW: Then getting her to shut up is not a strong enough objective. It can certainly get you started, but it's not going to take you through the entire experience.

C: I don't know what she would have to give me.

WW: It could be anything. If you could click your heels together three times and get your wish, what would it be?

C: That she wouldn't be against me.

WW: What's the opposite of her being against you?

C: Being on my side?

WW: Good! You want to change her opinion. You want to change her view of life, her view of the world.

C: Yes.

WW: And once you are able to do that, what do you want her to do?

C: To help me. To help me in my search.

WW: To stop being your enemy and start being your friend.

C: Well, that's going to be hard.

WW: Why?

C: Because she's really stuck in her ways.

WW: Then you're going to need all of your energy. You're going to have to really focus your thoughts and your work if you're going to accomplish your task. A truly resistant other is an actor's best friend.

Charlotte had created for herself a stubborn and powerful other, and in chapter 11, "Choosing an Other," we will spend more time looking at how you can make your other as potent an adversary as possible. The stronger the other, the stronger the action you will be required to take. Charlotte knew what she wanted and that the other she had chosen did not want to give it to her. She had done excellent work in creating her circumstance, and she now needed to spend more time taking the steps that would help her occupy that circumstance.

Once Charlotte took the time to move through each step of the centering process, she was able to occupy her circumstance in such a way that the only things that existed for her in that moment were her other and her need to get what she wanted from that other. She silenced the committee by finding something to do that was more powerful. She found something to do that was a lot more interesting than listening to the committee.

Over the next several weeks, Charlotte became really good at doing this work. She consistently and effectively occupied the dramatic circumstances she devised, and she then took powerful actions. The level of freedom with which Charlotte was working was really fun to watch.

WW: You actually appear to be having a good time.

C: I am!

WW: Why's that?

C: Well, everything's just gotten much simpler.

WW: Simpler how?

C: I know exactly what I have to do.

WW: And what's that?

C: I have to create my dragon, and then I have to slay it.

WW: I love that!

C: Me too.

WW: And slaying dragons is a lot more interesting than listening to a committee of people who are much less brave and talented than you are?

C: It is! And a whole lot more fun too!

Acting should be fun. Even when you are in the most dire of circumstances, acting is a way of exploring life experiences and feelings without actually being in any physical danger. It is not unlike taking a ride through a haunted house at an amusement park. You get genuinely scared, but you know that you are not in any real danger. When Meryl Streep, someone I think we can all agree knows a little something about acting, was interviewed on *Inside the Actors Studio*, she put it this way:

> We spend our whole lives as real human beings trying to get beyond the fears and the terrors that are everywhere for us, and to be an actor is to want to visit those dark places and the scary parts. I use it as a place to exorcise things that in my real life I would never want to have to deal with.

Another way to look at these two parts of the process: you engage your mind in order to create your story, and you engage your body in order to occupy the story that you have created.

7

Engaging
Your Instrument

The dramatic circumstance process outlined in this book shows you how to take specific steps to organize your thoughts so that you will be able to live more fully inside any story you choose to tell. As you utilize this process, you will begin to find yourself more and more able to bring any character more completely to life while also revealing yourself to the people who are watching you perform. Thus, it is through you that an audience will be able to recognize the characters you portray and will identify with those characters. That is what makes an audience care about the story and care about you.

We have also established that the most effective way for you to reveal yourself is to commit completely to the pursuit of an objective that you have discovered in your exploration of the dramatic circumstances you create and occupy. That *self* that you ultimately reveal will be comprised of the sounds you make, the physical actions you take, and the emotional connections you experience as you are living inside your dramatic circumstances and pursuing the things you want.

Beginning with chapter 9, "Finding a Problem," I will take a more detailed look at each component of the dramatic circumstance process and show you how you can get the most out of each of these components. If you are eager to delve deeper into those details right now, you should feel free to skip ahead. In this chapter and the next, however, I want to spend some time taking a look at the nuts and bolts of your physical instrument and the methods whereby you train it and keep it healthy. It is important that you learn as much as you can about the physical function of your voice and body. The way you train and care for your voice and body will have a major impact on your success, and there is no question that the efficient function of your physical instrument is vital to the longevity of your career. You need to learn how your instrument works, and you need to take care of it.

What exactly is your *instrument*? Your instrument is the totality of your body, mind, and spirit. In other words, it is an amalgamation of the physical, the mental, and the emotional components of you that come into play whenever you express yourself. While your instrument is not whole without all three of its components, it is only through the physical that you are actually able to communicate to other people. You have to make sounds, and you have to move. That is why I am taking this time to look more closely at the physical requirements and demands of the work you are doing.

First Do No Harm

One of the great benefits of having spent a lifetime working in music and theatre is that I have had the opportunity to know, work with, and learn from so many smart and talented people. I am particularly grateful for—and grateful to—the many voice teachers with whom I have had the pleasure of collaborating since joining the faculty at NYU. As I have listened to them and watched them work with our students, I have learned more about singing and singers than I ever thought I would know. The wisdom and expertise of these talented and dedicated colleagues has helped shape every aspect of the dramatic circumstance process as it is taught in the Steinhardt School and as it is being presented in this book.

That being said, as much as I have learned about singing over the past several years, I would never present myself as an authority in voice teaching, voice science, vocal health, or the intricacies of diaphragmatic breathing. I am an acting teacher and theatre director. My knowledge of the function of the voice and body comes from my own actor training and my own work experience. My knowledge also comes from observing the impact that I see my work have on the voices and physical expressiveness of the students with whom I do that work every day.

The work that I ask my students to do, and what I am asking you to do, presumes that you understand and are committed to good physical and vocal training. It also presumes that you are committed to providing yourself with a strong physical and vocal framework on which the successful functioning of your instrument depends. Performers, both the novice and the more experienced, are always subject to the possibility of physical strain or injury. Just because your physical instrument is capable of performing a particular function does not mean that it was meant to do it over and over again or for hours, days, and weeks at a time.

Performers often suffer from chronic physical problems that are the result of the ongoing stress they have imposed on their instruments. Anyone who does not utilize his or her voice and body wisely is susceptible to injury, but young performers often want to sound and perform as if they were much more experienced and physically mature than they actually are, and that puts them at particular risk. Damage can be done, and in some cases that damage can be permanent. Physical and vocal rehabilitation can take a long time and seriously impede your growth and progress. If, however, you are smart about the way you work and the way you care for your instrument, neither damage nor deterioration need be part of your life as a singer and actor.

I think that Hippocrates got it right, and those who work with performers should also adopt a "first do no harm" philosophy as a fundamental precept of the ethical training of singers and actors. A teacher should be aware of and guard against performers doing anything with their voices or bodies that causes unnecessary strain or might lead to any kind of damage. You as a performer need to develop that same awareness so that you can approach your work with care and caution. This chapter provides an overview of the way you engage and maintain your instrument, and the one following shows you how to utilize a healthy breathing technique in order to provide the fuel your instrument needs to keep it functioning in the most efficient and effective manner.

Again, I do not pretend to be expert in these areas. However, I can tell you that the information I am providing is physiologically sound and has demonstrated time and time again that it can help keep a singer on the straight and narrow when it comes to vocal function and health. I hope you will let this information influence the way you think about your body and your breath, and that you will commit yourself to a detailed study of your instrument. All professional singers and actors know that such study is essential to their physical health and vocal longevity.

The Craft of Making Art

You are an artist, and I assume that like any artist, specializing in any medium, you are committed to making art. Art, however, is not in and of itself the goal. Whenever "art" happens, if it happens at all, it is the result of a fortuitous coming together of what the artist is thinking and feeling, the steps the artist has taken as part of a clearly defined process, and the specific skills the artist has employed. Sometimes the day of the week, the weather, and the alignment of the planets also factor in.

What does the elusiveness of "art" mean for the performing artist? It means that you must focus on the process and not the product. Your process—any artist's process—consists of the steps you take and the thinking that inspires and guides those steps. In addition, the steps you take must always be supported by a carefully constructed foundation of highly developed skills that reflect your talent, your training, and your commitment to the work.

True ability for singers and actors manifests itself in the ease and efficiency with which they are able to perform the tasks associated with their art. Those tasks for a performer consist of taking physical actions and making sounds. You acquire ease and efficiency by learning the techniques that will lead to the optimum function of the various components of your instrument. Your job—your "do your work every day" job—is not to make art but to acquire, develop, and employ your skills. That set of skills becomes your technique. You must acquire your skills and practice them. It is through patience and practice that you develop your technique as a singer and as an actor.

Sometimes, usually in moments fueled by sudden inspiration, your skills may come together in such a fortuitous way that you actually do make art. Those are the good times. Those are the moments we work for and hope for, and when those moments happen, we treasure them. Your optimally functioning skills may well lead you to more and more of those inspired moments when all of the components of your work meld into a perfect whole. However, your technique is actually going to serve you best on those days when nothing seems to come together and that perfect whole seems miles away. Those are the days when your technique becomes essential for your very survival.

In the final analysis, art is always a by-product of whatever actions the artist may take. For singers and actors, those actions encompass a wide array of physical and emotional behaviors. As a performer, your art will always be a by-product of your ability to acquire and apply a specific set of skills. It is your job to learn those skills and, while doing so, make certain that your instrument is always able to function in a manner that makes those skills readily available for your use.

The Instrument Is You

You are your own instrument, and the components of that instrument are your mind, your body—which includes your literal voice—and your spirit. I use the word *spirit* in the context of this work because I feel it encompasses everything that makes up your figurative voice: the beliefs, needs, and emotions that motivate your behavior and give meaning to your actions. The goal is for your mind, body, and spirit to function together as an efficient and consistent whole. In other words, you must be able to engage all three components of your instrument whenever you want, and in order for that to happen on a regular basis, such as eight times a week, all three of these components must be trained.

My work as an acting teacher is concentrated in training the mind. I provide performers with a series of steps to follow—a specific way of organizing their thoughts—which connects them to their spirits. That connection is the thing that compels them to take action, thus engaging the body and voice. That is the thrust of the dramatic circumstance process.

How performers think, what they think, and when they think has a profound impact on what they are able to do. It is through the way that you organize and focus your thoughts as you breathe and center that you most effectively engage your body and your voice, and you have to practice in order to do that and do it consistently. We—not to mention the committee so often chattering away inside our heads—are naturally very good at distracting ourselves, and the goal of the dramatic circumstance process is to keep you so focused on what you need that your single-minded pursuit of your objective will keep those distractions at bay.

As a singer and actor, you use your brain to engage your body and consciousness in a complex set of coordinated functions that comprise what we ultimately see as performance. As a performer, your need for your brain and body to coordinate and come together in such precise ways is one of the biggest challenges you face. This coordination requirement of mind and body is both a blessing and a curse for those who choose to devote themselves to singing and acting. It is a blessing because of the exhilaration and satisfaction that can come from this coordination. It is a curse because the coordination itself can be elusive. It can take a long time to find and even longer to perfect, and if it is neglected, it can begin to slip away.

For many performers, this coordination of mind and body come together quite naturally. That natural coordination is what I think most people perceive as talent. A colleague of mine will often refer to a naturally gifted singer as having a "very talented throat." What he means is that a significant level of optimum vocal function comes quite naturally to that singer. In other words, some people are born with it. If you combine that level of natural function with an instinctive impulse to take action and a general lack of inhibition, the results can be quite impressive, and there is no arguing that some of the most impressive singers and actors we know have had little or no formal training. But let's not be led astray by the geniuses among us. It may well be that Barbra Streisand has never had a voice lesson or that Luciano Pavarotti could not read music, but I do not recommend that as a career strategy.

What is often mistaken for fully formed performance ability in a young performer is actually a talent for imitation. Your ability to sound like a famous singer can be a very good indicator that you have what it takes to ultimately find your own voice. However, in order to find your own voice, you are at some point going to have to give up the imitation. Every performer has a different degree of natural access to his or her instrument. At the top end of the spectrum, there are those gifted souls who appear to do it all with little or no effort. At the other end of the spectrum—or along the continuum where most of us reside—are singers who are in at least some part of their voices "stuck" or "locked." Regardless of where you may place yourself on this continuum of natural access to vocal coordination, I have found two things to be consistently true. First, access to optimum vocal function can shift dramatically from day to day or even moment to moment. Second, all singers, regardless of their natural ability, will benefit greatly from the same fundamental information about how their voices work and what they need to do to keep them working.

The thinking process I teach derives its impact and power from the fact that it shows you how to find within yourself a true impulse that will compel you to action. That is what makes this work both liberating and empowering. However, as free and powerful as you may feel when being compelled by your core instincts, your voice and body must be able to respond consistently and efficiently to those impulses. This is particularly true for those who work in live performance where the physical instrument is asked to engage and respond on schedule eight times a week. Connecting to your impulses and feeling empowered by those impulses is an important first step. Knowing how to utilize your impulses efficiently and consistently while still taking good care of your instrument takes some time.

Training the Instrument

Successful athletes and successful singers have a lot in common. They engage in strenuous physical activity, and they understand that physical training is an essential component in the effective expression of their "art." While I do believe that it is through your mind that you gain access to all of your performance skills, you must never lose sight of the fact that singing and acting are physical activities. Your body—your actual physical being—will undoubtedly be influenced by your thoughts and feelings, but your physical body can also have a great impact on the way you think and feel. The ultimate test of a performer's ability—and, I believe, the key to that performer's success—is how effectively the mind and body are able to function together. The train-your-brain process laid out in this book is the most effective way I have found for you to engage and explore your own instincts and abilities, and when you fully engage those instincts and abilities, you reveal your power not only to others—namely, the people who might admire you and hire you—but also to yourself.

Most of the students I encounter do believe in their own fundamental talent, but they have little idea of their own power. It would be an understatement to say that it is exciting to watch them discover it. But as exciting as it may be, the power that derives from the full engagement of your talent and instincts cannot by itself take you as far as you want to go for as long as you want to go there. Careers built solely on talent and instinct can be very impressive. They can also be limited in their scope and are often short lived. Instincts can elude you. Limitations of range can reveal themselves. Bodies and voices will tire and give out. That is why good training is essential. It does not create talent, but it does nurture and protect it.

You will always do your best singing and your best acting when your mind, body, and voice are fully engaged and working together. Knowing how to effectively, efficiently, and consistently engage and coordinate these faculties will be the foundation of your work and, I hope, the foundation of your career.

A Manifesto for the Voice

The effective application of the dramatic circumstance process depends upon your ability to apply the fundamental principles of a healthy vocal technique. One of your foremost responsibilities to yourself as a singer is to have consistent access to your vocal instrument and to the range of notes, dynamics, and colors that your specific voice is capable of producing. There are three essential components that make up what I consider to be optimum vocal function:

- You must be able to *breathe effectively and efficiently*, thus providing your vocal apparatus with the fuel it needs in order to function.

- You must be able to *rid yourself of extraneous muscle tension* so that your body can support the most efficient use of your breath and you can maintain even airflow through the vocal folds.
- You must be able to *achieve and sustain a level of mask resonance* that will produce your most vibrant sound and provide you with the easiest access to the words you sing.

Mask resonance is experienced by singers as vibration or a sensation of "buzz" in the cheekbones and nasal passages. Good breath energy and airflow create the sensation that the voice has moved "forward" and out of the throat. Singers who maintain a forward resonance usually experience their singing as "easier" or "brighter." The ability to sing with forward resonance, which is also referred to as singing "in the mask," is particularly important to music theatre singers who are generally expected to produce a brighter sound. I happen to believe that forward resonance is also the friend of classical singers, but that conversation is not the subject of this book.

Why is resonance so important? Resonance is what allows a voice to carry the farthest and be heard most clearly. Many singers push their voices and struggle to achieve volume or an "edgier" sound when resonance is the thing they need. Resonance that is the result of proper placement and good airflow will make a voice sound much bigger and more powerful while at the same time protecting the health of the vocal apparatus.

A Manifesto for the Body

When you organize your thoughts, your entire mechanism will become more focused and fully engaged. It is then that your body, your physical instrument, will be able to respond immediately and efficiently to any impulse you have to take an action. It only makes sense that in order for this to happen, your body must be in its best condition. I have also broken down the state of optimum physical function into its three core components:

- You must be able to *breathe effectively and efficiently*, thus providing your body with the fuel it needs to function.
- You must *maintain a level of physical strength*, the product of regular exercise and healthy habits that will give you the stamina you need to perform.
- You must *have flexibility of movement* so that your body can respond quickly and freely to any impulse you have to take action.

The components for optimum function of voice and body are very similar, which only makes sense. The two are inextricably linked, and their needs are similar. I advise you to get to know your voice and your body. Ask them to work hard for you, and help them to do that by giving them everything they need. They will return the favor by giving you years of healthy physical function and a great deal of pleasure.

Planning and Practice

You have probably heard this very old joke. A young man approaches a homeless person in midtown New York and asks, "How do you get to Carnegie Hall?" The street person shouts, "Practice!"

For the performer, practice can be defined as the time you spend by yourself working to apply the instructions you have received from your teacher. Those who study singing and acting—who may be working simultaneously with a voice teacher, an acting teacher, a vocal coach, a musical director, a director, and a choreographer— are often trying to apply instructions they have received from more than one person. How you take in and incorporate all those instructions will play a critical role in how successfully you make the changes that will have the greatest impact on your singing and acting and, ultimately, your performance.

You have to be willing to accept and implement instruction. That may sound self-evident, but I have to say that I am still surprised at the number of students who resist hearing what a teacher is saying or are reluctant to give something a try. I also have to say that I am still impressed by the variety of creative ways in which some students manage to avoid both listening to and following instructions. There is, of course, a level of trust that must develop between any student and any teacher, and I understand that it may take some time to establish that trust. I do not believe that a questioning mind or a healthy skepticism have ever interfered with a student's learning. On the contrary, students should not be expected to accept without question everything their teachers tell them. That, however, is different than not being willing to follow an instruction in order to find out what might happen when you do. If you honestly don't believe that what a teacher is telling you is in your best interests, and you believe that you have been open and honest in your communication and given your student-teacher relationship a full measure of time, then you are well within your rights to go elsewhere. In the classes I teach, a semester is fourteen weeks, and I don't think that fourteen weeks is too long a time for me to expect a student to try the things I am suggesting and talk honestly about his or her experience. I recognize that students are impatient. You want results, and you want them now. Make sure, however, that in your pursuit of excellence and success, both of which are admirable things, you are not so focused on the results you want to achieve that you are unable to take the kind of incremental steps that might ultimately lead you to those very results.

Assuming that you have implemented an instruction into your work, it is of vital importance that you be able to articulate for your teacher and yourself what impact you feel that instruction has had on what you were doing. This is the way in which you and your teacher develop a shared vocabulary, and it facilitates a way of communicating that will both enhance your growth and reinforce the changes you are making. It is also the way that you and your teacher can determine which instructions and which articulation of those instructions are the most effective for you. Every student is an individual, and while we work within what I believe are many fundamental and universal concepts, the way you experience and articulate your work will always belong to you. That is as it should be.

If you take an instruction, apply it to the best of your ability, and follow that with an honest conversation with your teacher, you are going to be able to make significant changes in your singing and your acting. This part of the process may take place in a lesson, a class, or a rehearsal. However, the ongoing application of those instructions takes place when you are on your own, when you practice. How you practice and how much you practice will determine how successful you are going to be.

There was a study done several years ago in England that examined the background and education of successful musicians. The researchers were trying to determine if there were significant factors in the social, economic, or cultural background of these musicians that influenced their success. When the data was analyzed, it was discovered that the only statistically significant factor that had any impact on the success of these performers was the amount of time they had spent practicing. So it is a fact: the more you practice, the better you will get.

Figuring out just how to practice is one of the biggest challenges most performers face. Without the guiding voice of the teacher or coach, it is easy to lose track of just what you are doing and just what you are meant to be thinking about. In my experience, for most performers, what interferes most with effective practice is a tendency to try to do too many things at the same time.

Ideally you will reach the point with any piece of performance material when your mind, body, and voice will function together with almost no conscious awareness of the work they are doing or how they are working together. That is when that piece will be ready to perform. However, while you are preparing to perform, you must decide which particular part of your instrument you are going to "exercise" and what particular performance skills you are going to practice. For example, you might be in a practice session and decide, "I am going to work on my airflow." You then take yourself through the exercises and the phrases of music that you have worked on with your teacher, and you endeavor to recreate the sensation you found in your lesson that confirms for you that your air is moving just the way you want it to move. You might next decide, "I am going to maintain forward resonance through this phrase," and again try to achieve the sensation of resonance that you were able to achieve when you were working with your teacher.

The key to effective practice is knowing that it is impossible to do everything at the same time. While it is your goal that the components of your instrument ultimately work together, you cannot bring them together through the force of your will. My advice is that you pick one thing, and that you work on that one thing until you feel you have gained facility in that particular area.

You then pick something else and work on that. Only when you feel that you have spent the requisite amount of time on the specific skills required for the material on which you are working do you decide to explore how efficiently those skills come together as you perform. I consider "performance" to be that time in your practice when you commit fully to your dramatic circumstance, and in those instances, you evaluate your success in terms of how effectively you were able to commit to the pursuit of your objective.

The various components that make up the whole of any successful performance absolutely do need to function simultaneously. Those components, however, do not work together simply because you decide to take responsibility for all of them at the same time. On the contrary, all too often I see performers get frustrated simply because they have taken on too many tasks at one time. Your desire to succeed—to get it right—can make you impatient, and being impatient with yourself is not helpful. Commit to your process and the individual steps that make up that process. Things will start to come together. I promise.

Embrace "Technique"

The word *technique* is used a lot in the study of singing and acting, and I have found that singers and actors tend to think about technique somewhat differently. Singers seem to more readily accept the idea that there are basic physical functions essential to the effective practice of their craft and that those functions need to be identified and practiced. Actors tend to be more resistant to the idea that anything as mundane as technical, physical proficiency is going to play a significant role in their performance, and singing actors can be trapped between those two points of view. While they are willing to commit to the detailed physical training they know their work requires, they do not want to feel encumbered by that training when the moment arrives for them to actually perform.

Describing someone as a good "technician" does seem to imply that the person is something less of an artist. To describe someone's acting or singing as "technical" is a way of saying that while all of the pieces of the performance are in place, those pieces are assembled in only an intellectual way. Therefore, the resulting performance lacks the more desirable qualities of inspiration, spontaneity, and emotional connection.

When I began my acting studies in New York in the mid-1970s, it was considered a given that English actors were more "technical" while American actors were more "method." The word *method* in this context referred to any kind of emotionally based actor training. Actors were thought of as belonging to one school of thought or the other. You were either a method actor working from the inside out or you were a technique-based actor working from the outside in. I doubt, however, if the difference in the two approaches, particularly in the way that any individual actor went about his or her work, was ever that distinct. Even so, this is a conversation that I still hear take place among my students who are working so hard to sing and act at the same time. Unfortunately, this kind of thinking contributes to a general misconception that when you are singing you are doing one thing and when you are acting you are doing another.

In the final analysis, the process of learning how to bring characters to life when you are acting and singing at the same time is not as simple as just picking one approach or another. There are many different ways to learn about the function of your body, voice, psyche, and soul, and any one of these ways may provide you at any given moment with the best and most consistent access to your particular set of performance skills. Most singers and actors I work with, and you are probably no exception, say that they want their work to come from "inside" rather than "outside." You want your work to be emotionally connected and true, and you do not want your behavior dictated by external expectations that distract you from your intentions. While I do understand this point of view, I don't believe that acting is ever an either/or proposition. To think of your emotional life as somehow "inside" while your physical life is "outside" is already a perception that denies the complex interaction between the various parts of your mind and your body. Your emotional self and your physical self are forever intertwined and totally dependent on each other. Learning how they interact and how to make the best use of that interaction is one of the most challenging and rewarding aspects of any performer's work.

Of course you want to find a true emotional connection in your work, and the dramatic circumstance process is the most effective way I have found to bring that about. Even so, emotionally connected work will be diminished, and your ability to sustain it will be seriously compromised, if your body and voice are not at the same time functioning both efficiently and effectively. And I think that *efficient* and *effective* are the best words to describe work that is built on a foundation of good technique.

So just what is technique? Technique is the facility with which you are able to consistently access and engage your voice, body, and mind—the basic components of your instrument.

How do you develop your technique? You develop your technique through thoughtful training and patient practice.

8

Supplying the Fuel

A few years ago, I read a magazine interview with Mel Gibson about a big new movie he had directed that had been shot on location with many local people playing major roles. The interviewer asked if working with nonprofessionals had been a problem, and Mel answered, "Anyone who can breathe can act." At first I thought that Mel was just being a smart aleck and dismissing the question, but the more I thought about it, the more I realized he was saying something that was absolutely true. A full, low, energized breath is a powerful starting place for anything that any performer sets out to do, regardless of that performer's training or experience, and when a performer employs breath in such a conscious and specific manner, many interesting things will start to happen.

What starts to happen? In my experience, the body and voice will respond quite naturally to whatever impulse comes along for that performer to move or speak. Furthermore, the performer will begin to communicate from a place that seems to somehow come from deeper within the consciousness, lower in the body. People who are fully connected to their breath are much more physically free, and they somehow appear to be telling the truth. Remember that Stanislavski told us that good acting was about behaving truthfully in an imaginary circumstance. If breathing worked for the locals in Mel's movie, it can work for you.

I know I am not alone in believing that the way you breathe, the way in which air enters and leaves your body, is the single most significant factor in your growth and development as a singer and as an actor. I think it is so important that I once told a class that if I were to give them a written exam on any subject, they could fill in any blank with the word *breathe* and I would give them half credit. Efficient, effective breathing supplies the fuel that allows your instrument to function. It supplies oxygen to your brain and your body, and it creates the flow of air that sets up the vibration that produces sound. Without it, you have nothing, and it is imperative that you develop and maintain good breathing habits.

There is an abundance of material available that describes in great detail the process of diaphragmatic breathing. There are books, pamphlets, videos, and web links that can help you understand how the breathing process works, why it works, and why it is essential for both your performance and your health. What I am providing in this chapter is a basic overview of the way your respiratory system functions. Along with that information, I am describing specific steps you can take in order to utilize that function to the greatest benefit for both your singing and your acting. Your breath is what will get the instrument going, and a good breathing technique provides the means for you to seamlessly amalgamate your acting with your singing.

The Apparatus

Deep breathing, most often referred to as *diaphragmatic breathing*, is the most effective way for a performer to breathe. It is, in fact, the most effective way for anyone to breathe at any time. Most of us breathe shallowly. This tends to be true even for trained singers and actors as they go about their everyday lives. We do not allow the lungs to fully expand, and because of that, the lungs do not actually fill with air. It deprives the body of oxygen and causes the muscles and organs to have to work harder. Shallow breathing and rapid breathing are also common reactions to stress, and since stress is familiar territory for performers, shallow breathing is often the first obstacle that singers and actors must learn to overcome as they practice and perform.

In an effort to get students to take a deep breath so that they can experience the powerful impact of diaphragmatic breathing, teachers will often employ various kinds of imagery. You may have been told to "breathe into your gut" or even to "breathe into the soles of your feet." I hope you realize that neither of those things is physically possible. Imagery intended to inspire a low breath may be helpful, but it can sometimes lead to confusion as to how the respiratory system actually functions.

The air you breathe into your body comes into your lungs— nowhere else. The oxygen in the air you breathe moves into your bloodstream and travels to all parts of your body, but the air itself comes only into your lungs. Your rib cage encloses the thoracic cavity, and it provides protection for the vital organs of the thorax. Those vital organs are your heart and your lungs. The thorax must expand and contract in order for you to breathe, and the most effi- cient way for this to happen involves the opening of the chest, the dropping down of the diaphragm, and the expansion of the ribs.

Your diaphragm is a large parachute-shaped muscle that bisects your thoracic cavity. It is attached to the bottom of your ribcage and sits on top of your stomach. It is connected in the front where your ribs come together, along the sides of your lower ribs and along your back. Your diaphragm has a central tendon that attaches to the connective tissue surrounding your lungs. When you take a breath, your brain sends a signal to the diaphragm. The diaphragm's muscle fibers contract and pull down the central tendon. This pushes your "belly organs" out of the way so that your lungs have more room to expand. Most people think of the diaphragm as sitting much lower in the body than it actually does, and that misconception can interfere with effective diaphragmatic breathing. Take a minute now to run your fingers along the bottom of both sides of your rib cage until they meet in the middle of your chest. This is the spot where your diaphragm connects in the front, and it is the place where you should feel your abdomen expanding as you take in air.

When you inhale, the diaphragm pulls down, and the rib cage expands outward to the sides. This expansion reduces the pressure inside your chest cavity, creating a vacuum. In order to equalize the pressure, this vacuum draws air into your lungs through the trachea, also known as your windpipe. This is inhalation. Many people think of the expansion that comes with inhalation as being the result of the air pushing the diaphragm down and the ribs apart. In fact, what happens is the opposite of that. It is by pulling down the diaphragm and expanding the ribs that you actually draw air into your body.

As you exhale, the diaphragm relaxes. The air flows out, and the rib cage returns to its resting position. It is the air moving out of your body that causes the vocal folds to vibrate. That vibration of the vocal folds is how sound is produced whenever you speak or sing, and that production of sound is called *phonation*.

The way singers experience the air moving in and out of their bodies can vary greatly from individual to individual. We know how the respiratory system functions, just as we know how your vocal apparatus produces sound. Your individual experience, however, of breathing and phonating is the key to your own growth. Your personal experience of how diaphragmatic breathing works for you is what needs to be explored, articulated, and practiced.

You must consciously practice the way you breathe. A teacher can show you how it works. However, it is your own awareness and mastery of your breath that will enable you to take full advantage of the benefits of an efficient breathing technique, and that is work you have to do yourself.

Centering

Your breath is intrinsically connected to the function of both your autonomic nervous system and your brain. Thus the benefits of good breathing are both physical and psychological. Gaining the most benefit from effective breathing technique requires that you become aware of the specific steps you must take in order for your breath to empower you both physically and psychologically. This work, this process of engaging your breath while aligning your body and your mind in order to focus and prepare yourself to act and sing, is referred to as *centering*. Centering yourself is the method through which you will achieve the greatest access to the power of your breath as well as the strongest connection to your dramatic circumstances. The centering process requires that you take yourself through three distinct phases.

Phase One: Stand Tall and Breathe Deep

Begin by standing with your feet about shoulder width apart and your toes pointed straight forward. Allow your spine to lengthen.

For many people, it helps to imagine that there is a string attached to a point at the very top of your head and that the string is gently lifting you upward.

Release your jaw. The best way to experience this sensation is to lightly rest your fingers on each side of your face right at the point where your jaw hinges. Let the jaw drop just far enough that your mouth opens slightly. Many people in an attempt to release the jaw will start overworking it or trying to push it down. That is not the idea. It is a gentle release that should create the sensation that your jaw is hanging slightly down from your skull. There should be a space between your teeth about as wide as the tip of your little finger.

Allow yourself to breathe with a conscious awareness of the dropping down of your diaphragm and the expansion of your rib cage. Your chest opens, and your shoulders remain down and relaxed. As you inhale and exhale, it is natural for the chest to move up and down a bit. Some singers fixate on keeping the chest from moving at all, and this can lead to a kind of collapse in the upper body, which interferes with both breathing and resonance. Allow the chest to move naturally. The goal is for your chest and body to stay open and long. Open means that there is as much space as possible between the shoulders, and long refers to the entire spine from your tailbone to your neck. There should also be a sense of lengthening from your navel to your sternum.

Phase Two: Measure and Focus

Breathe in gently on a count of four and breathe out on a count of six. This nice, even flow of breath, called *measured breathing*, will help you bring yourself more fully into the actual room you are in, and from this place of heightened awareness of your surroundings, you should take the time to explore the sensory experience of where you are. Feel the temperature. Feel the air moving across your skin. Be aware of the amount of light in the room and any particular quality that light may have. Hear any sounds that may be happening around you.

One of the biggest challenges most performers face is being fully present in the room. This can be true in classes and rehearsals, but it is particularly true in auditions. You can utilize measured breathing as a way to practice becoming more present in any room you happen to occupy, and when you have practiced this enough, you will be able to quickly and fully occupy any space under any circumstances. It can be a lifesaver.

From this place of measured breathing, you next select a point of focus somewhere directly in front of you at about eye level or a bit higher. As you inhale, imagine you are gently pulling energy from that point of focus directly into your body. As you exhale, imagine you are sending that energy back to your point of focus.

Phase Three: Keep Breathing and Center

You are physically aligned, breathing deeply and evenly, and you are fully present in the room. You are now ready to connect to your physical *center*. Rest your thumbs lightly on your navel. Let your fingertips drop down about three inches, and gently press them into that spot in your lower abdomen. Imagine that your breath energy is flowing into that specific point in your body as you inhale and flowing out from that point as you exhale. That point in your lower abdomen below your navel is what we identify as your center, and over time you will come to recognize that spot as the source of the power you need to do your work.

Centering is the process whereby you utilize deep, measured, and focused breathing in order to reach a place of heightened awareness and activate that core spot in your lower abdomen that we have identified as your center. This process is invaluable to any performer and should always be a part of your practice, rehearsal, and performance regimen. You can easily practice this technique several times throughout the day and in a variety of situations. With regular practice, the centering response becomes virtually automatic, and you will find yourself able to focus in a matter of seconds. You will also find it a useful technique that can be applied in any number of situations, not only in singing and acting but also in life.

The amount of time you need to spend in each of the three centering phases will depend on the level of proficiency you are able to attain in each phase. It will also be affected by the state you and your instrument are in on any given day and the specific material on which you are working. In other words, centering is an active, always-evolving process. The specific way you go about it and the time it takes for you to reach a centered place in any rehearsal or performance situation is something that you will be able to gauge over time as you gain both skill and experience.

Dramatic Centering

In the chapters that follow, we will take a more detailed look at each component of a dramatic circumstance. You will see in each instance how the performer finds a very specific language that is then incorporated into the centering process in order to fully occupy his or her particular circumstances. That is the part of the process that I refer to as *dramatic centering*. Dramatic centering is what allows you to utilize the power of your centered state to bring your circumstances to life. It is the critical step you take in order to occupy and live inside the story you are telling in each song you sing.

Just how do you do that? Consider the work that Katerina did with "Where Is Love?" She directed her sensory focus to the cold, lonely room in which she found herself imprisoned, and through her articulation of her problem and envisioning of her other, she was able to find the very specific language of her objective. Katerina was able to fully occupy the dramatic circumstance that she created for the person who was going to ask the question "Where is love?" She used her imagination to create her story in terms that meant something to her, and she used her breath and focus to step inside that story and sing to her mother.

It is important to keep in mind that centering is not meditation. Meditation and other consciousness-raising or relaxation techniques do employ the same kind of breathing process, but the dramatic centering process is not intended to disconnect you from reality— far from it. Dramatic centering allows you to step into another reality of your own choosing so that you can operate from within that reality while still being aware that you are present in the classroom, studio, or stage that you actually occupy. You utilize dramatic centering to make yourself more fully present in the circumstance you have envisioned.

One real benefit of working this way—and why this approach to acting works so well for singers—is that while your breath is working so efficiently, your body will be relaxed. In this relaxed but engaged physical state, you can experience yourself as being highly energized and eager to pursue your objective without that excitement creating extraneous tension. We can never eliminate all tension from our bodies, nor do we want to. Without tension, the stretching and tightening of your muscles, your body will not actually be able to function. The tensions you do want to eliminate, or at least minimize, are those that interfere with your ability to stand upright and access the energy you need to make a sound or take an action.

Your goal in this preparation process is to achieve a state of *anticipatory stillness.* In this state, you are breathing deeply. You are relaxed but with a sense of energy radiating from an activated core. You are keenly aware of everything that is going on in your body, and you are aware of what is happening around you. From this readied place, you are drawing powerful information from your mind, your body, and your emotions. You are thus prepared to take any action that your circumstance might require.

Centering, like everything else you are trying to incorporate into your work, is something that you get better at as time goes by and the more you practice. Take the time to center several times a day in any variety of situations. Anytime it occurs to you that you can center, just do it and see what happens. See if in those moments you begin to experience your environment in a different way, in a more present way. At the same time, see if you experience yourself as more present, more energized, or more active, with a sense that something might happen and that anything can happen.

Why can anything happen? Because you are totally present in your physical surroundings and fully engaged in the story you are telling. You are fully present in a world that is filled with stimuli and can change quickly. You are at the center of a world that you have created.

"Go *East,* Young Man"

I will take the liberty of paraphrasing Horace Greeley (who was already paraphrased when quoted as having told his apocryphal young man to "go West") and suggest that you turn your attention Eastward. It has taken a long time, but Western medicine and culture do seem to acknowledge the importance of breath and body connection to a person's mental and physical health, and the validity of the many disciplines that explore those connections. There are any number of Eastern philosophies and body practices that are based on how we come to recognize and utilize the way that energy flows through our bodies and how that energy can be used to our benefit.

In the practice of yoga, taking just one example of an Eastern body practice that is taught in almost every city in the United States, the energy point that we connect to in the centering process is identified as the *second chakra*. Among the functions and qualities associated with the second chakra are emotion, sexuality, desire, pleasure, and procreation. Those very human functions and qualities are without question the "stuff" of dramatic circumstance, and the energy derived from that centered place in our bodies is both sensual (of the senses) and emotional (of the instincts and intuition). In other words, the dramatic centering process through which we use breath and body to occupy the story we are telling is also how we utilize mind and body to access our spirits and our hearts.

Words to Live By

A respiratory therapist I know wears a T-shirt that reads, "If you can't breathe, nothing else matters!" I suggest that you adapt that phrase *ever so* slightly and adopt it *oh so* completely.

If you *don't* breathe, nothing else matters.

9

Finding a Problem

At the center of any good story, there is a person with a problem. When someone starts to tell us a story, it is that problem that captures our attention. Then it is the way the story's central character goes about solving his or her problem that completely pulls us in. A good story needs a person, a problem, and an attempt to solve that problem. As an actor, it is your job to assume the role of the central character in each story you tell and to set out to solve that person's problem. In order to do that you have to identify the problem, and you have to identify *with* the problem.

What does it mean to have a problem? Having a problem simply means that there is something you are experiencing in your life that you want or need to be different than it is. You will begin to notice that you have a problem whenever a want or need becomes strong enough to start making you uncomfortable. A problem calls attention to itself. It is a thought that enters your head and distracts or worries you, or a physical sensation of which you suddenly become aware. Obviously, problems exist in varying degrees of intensity and will create varying levels of discomfort. Most of the problems that arise throughout the course of a day you would not even identify as problems. There are all sorts of minor imbalances and adjustments that occur in our lives that get addressed immediately and solved within minutes—typical things like hunger, thirst, or needing to go to the bathroom. The problems that make for good stories are the ones that are not so easy to solve, and for an actor, the most useful problems are the ones that make you the most uncomfortable. It is those problems that will elicit your strongest, most specific, and most interesting behavior.

The English have a word they use when they are totally shocked or utterly astonished. The word is *gobsmacked*. Its literal definition is "shocked by a blow to the mouth," but it is used to describe a state of being so completely surprised that it feels as if one has been hit in the face, smacked in the gob. In addition to appreciating the sound of the word, the way the consonants slap up against each other, I like it because it specifically describes an emotional reaction in physical terms. It expresses a level of surprise that creates physical sensation. Furthermore, it allows for the surprise to be happy or unhappy or a little bit of both.

For the purposes of this work, I describe any heightened emotional experience, be it pleasant or unpleasant, as *problematic*, because along with any emotional experience, there is always some degree of physical sensation. Whether the physical sensation is one you like or do not like, it still calls attention to itself. It creates an imbalance in your physical and psychological mechanism, and it must be addressed. From that perspective, losing the love of your life and finding the love of your life are both equally problematic. The emotional experience of losing and the emotional experience of winning, even though one feels better than the other, both create a physical experience that must be addressed. And the fact that this emotional/physical sensation must be addressed, that it cannot be ignored, makes it a problem.

It is essential that you recognize how useful it can be to begin to think of your emotional life in terms of physical sensation. This will, in fact, become one of your most powerful working tools. Learning to articulate your emotional reaction to a circumstance in terms of physical discomfort is the key to incorporating your problem state into your centering process and, thusly, into your performance.

In addition to conveying an actual sensation of physical discomfort, an effective problem must be personal enough to spark your imagination. The problem must resonate in your imagination and consciousness so strongly that you will be compelled to *live* within the circumstance of the story. In order for that to happen, your problem must speak to you in a vocabulary that means something personal to you. That is what the "what if" game is intended to do. You use it to place yourself in the middle of a problematic situation so that you can more readily identify your own responses to that situation. The bottom line is that you want to articulate your problem in a manner that is so compelling that you have no choice but to do something about it.

A physically discombobulating problem and a strong personal identification with that problem are the two things that will make your dramatic circumstances both immediate and alive. For an actor, taking a piece of material and identifying and articulating your problem in these terms is like striking gold.

Coaching: Finding the Problem

Behavior within a dramatic circumstance often makes sense only to the person who is actually in that circumstance, and you cannot effectively analyze from outside the circumstance. You will only be able to step inside a story when you let yourself imagine the situation as if it were your own. The quickest way to go about this is to adopt the perspective of the person who is singing the song. Once Katerina asked herself, "What if I were cold and hungry and locked up and unloved?" her imagination began to bring her story to life. This is the process whereby any song will become uniquely yours.

The following coaching is an example of how a singer investigates his situation in order to find his most immediate, powerful problem. He then takes the work a step further by exploring his circumstance and making his problem large enough to compel him to take an action. The student is Kevin, and the goal of this coaching is for Kevin to articulate his problem in as concise, complete, and personal a manner as possible. The song is "All the Things You Are"—a ballad by Jerome Kern and Oscar Hammerstein II in which the singer tries to find the most poetic and lyrical way to express what it means to him to have found true love.

WW: What is your problem?

K: My girlfriend doesn't know how much I love her.

WW: And why is that a problem?

K: Because I do love her.

WW: Then why don't you just tell her?

K: That's what I'm going to do in the song.

WW: Why take the time to sing a whole song if all you have to do is say, "I love you"? That takes about two seconds and would save everybody a lot of time.

K: Well, I have to sing the song.

WW: Only because you're in a class that's about singing songs.

K: What?

WW: Your reason to sing can't be just because you've been assigned a song. Once you begin to sing, you aren't here in class. You are supposed to be with your girlfriend, and in that scenario—that story—you have to figure out why you would sing this song to her.

K: To tell her I love her.

WW: That's too easy! A problem can't simply be un-finished business—something you can accomplish by just saying the words. A good working problem—one that's going to provide you with some real motivation—needs to require some effort to solve. It needs to be something that is going to compel you to take an action.

K: That's what's so hard about this song!

WW: What's hard?

K: All it really says is "I love you."

WW: I agree, but it says that in a pretty big way.

K: Tell me about it. It's so romantic and poetic.

WW: Then you need to find a pretty big romantic and poetic reason to sing it, and that means you need a pretty big problem.

K: I know. I just can't find one!

WW: Why not?

K: Because I'm happy! I love my girlfriend. She loves me.

WW: You're sure about that?

K: I need her to tell me that she loves me?

WW: That's a start. How will you get her to do that?

K: Sing the song?

WW: Sing it lovingly? Sing with all your heart? Show her how much you care?

K: That doesn't sound very interesting.

WW: I agree. And nobody said you had to sing this to your actual girlfriend.

K: But I thought we were supposed to use personal circumstances.

WW: You want to use circumstances that resonate with you—things that strike a chord because you understand them or have had them actually happen to you. Can you remember the first time you fell in love...seriously in love?

K: Uh...yeah.

WW: What was it like?

K: Well...whenever I was around her I got really nervous.

WW: Did she love you back?

K: That was the thing. I didn't know, and I couldn't figure out how to find out.

WW: So what happened?

K: It got to where I couldn't sleep...couldn't eat.

WW: That doesn't sound like any fun.

K: Well, I lost five pounds. That was good.

WW: And you were happy?

K: No. I was miserable...really uncomfortable. Like I'd been hit in the head.

WW: Great. When you got to the word *uncomfortable*, you moved into problem vocabulary. As you took the time to envision a circumstance by remembering the first time you fell in love, you were able to arrive—very quickly, I might point out—at a point in that circumstance where you experienced a problem.

K: That I was uncomfortable.

WW: Problems—in the way that we are talking about them—are levels of discomfort, an actual sense of physical discombobulation.

K: Well, I was certainly discombobulated.

WW: Right. But were you still happy that you were in love?

K: Sure. Now that I think about. It was all part of the whole mixed-up thing.

WW: So were you happy being uncomfortable?

K: No. I was in love. Uncomfortable just came with the territory.

WW: Because you were having these feelings and didn't know if she felt the same way.

K: Right.

WW: So your problem didn't derive from whether you were happy or unhappy.

K: I get it.

WW: What did your problem derive from?

K: Whether I was comfortable or uncomfortable.

WW: If you think that way, you won't have any trouble finding a problem.

As I wrote in the beginning of this chapter, an actor begins the process of creating a dramatic circumstance by clearly articulating a state of discomfort. That does not mean that the state of discomfort—the problem—has to be a state of unhappy discomfort. It could just as easily be a state of joyful discomfort. There are many moments in many stories when someone suddenly realizes that he or she has fallen in love, and there are many songs in which that overwhelming realization is the event that is taking place. It is likely that the person to whom this is happening is going to find the experience at least somewhat discombobulating. Too many things are happening at one time. There are more questions filling your brain than there are answers. This discombobulated state, even though it is not an unhappy one, can easily make you so uncomfortable that you want to do something about it. That is the point when discomfort becomes a problem that you have to address. The point is not the kind of discomfort but the level of discomfort. In developing your dramatic circumstance, it is most important that your "un-comfortableness" reach a level that compels you to take an action.

WW: You're in a situation that is causing you discomfort. How can you solve it?

K: By telling her that I love her and getting her to tell me that she loves me back.

WW: What if she doesn't love you back?

K: That wouldn't be good.

WW: Would the possibility of her not loving you back be on your mind when you told her that you loved her?

K: Yeah, I guess it would.

WW: So what's your problem now?

K: Uncomfortable and...scared?

WW: Anyone would be scared if he were declaring his love with no assurance of what kind of response he was going to get. An audience watching that event take place will identify with the person who is making that declaration.

K: And that's a good thing?

WW: It couldn't hurt.

K: So...now I have a problem.

WW: And a need to sing the song.

K: Right.

WW: Do you have a big enough need?

K: Big enough for what?

WW: Big enough to sing words like "You are the promised kiss of springtime"?

K: Er...not when you put it that way.

WW: Why not?

K: Because those words are...too much? She'd probably think I was crazy, and I'd end up scaring her away.

WW: So...we need a bigger problem to support the "bigger" language.

Kevin has found a problem—in fact, two problems—that would absolutely help bring his song into focus. They would not, however, allow this particular song to come to life either musically or lyrically in the way I think the authors intended. These words and this music are more expansive and expressive than the circumstance and problem with which Kevin is currently working.

WW: You're singing to a girl that you love.

K: Right.

WW: So let's keep working with your story so that it will support the language of the song. What situation would make you work as hard— would make you commit to language as much as the singer of this song is clearly committed?

K: Well...it's not my first love.

WW: Why not?

K: I think I'd have to know the girl pretty well.

WW: Why's that?

K: Because I wouldn't say these words to someone I didn't know. It's like...reciting poetry.

WW: And you're not likely to recite poetry to a girl you're just getting to know.

K: Correct. Not at all likely.

WW: So...poetry is not in your nature.

K: Definitely not.

WW: But it's not beyond you.

K: No.

WW: Is there any kind of situation that would make you use language like this?

K: It would have to be really important.

WW: Like...?

K: Like if I were asking her to marry me.

WW: Okay. What would your problem be then?

K: I'd be scared out of my mind.

WW: Scared of what?

K: Scared of her saying no...or her saying yes. Scared of making that kind of commitment.

WW: But she does love you and will probably say yes.

K: I think so...this is just a "what if," right?

WW: Right. And we're looking for the "what if" that puts you at the greatest risk.

K: She could be mad at me.

WW: That's a step in the right direction.

K: Okay. My problem is that my girlfriend is mad at me.

WW: No. That's your situation. I agree that there is the potential for a problem in that situation, but you still need to find it and name it.

K: How?

WW: Do you care that your girlfriend is mad at you?

K: Sure. Of course I care.

WW: Nothing in the analysis process is ever "sure" or "of course." You must articulate exactly what is happening. How do I know you care? More importantly, how do you know that you care? The statement "My girlfriend is mad at me" could easily be followed by "...and I don't give a damn!"

K: But I do give a damn.

WW: So then...what is your problem?

K: My girlfriend is mad at me, and I'm really upset about it.

I frequently coach the Irving Berlin song "Supper Time," a song being sung by a woman who has just received word that her husband has been killed. When I ask the singer what her problem is, she will invariably tell me that her husband is dead. As logical as that answer may seem to be, the dead husband is not, in fact, her problem. The dead husband is her situation, her circumstance. In order to find her problem, she has to consider the various ways in which a woman might respond to the news of her husband's death. I can think of any number of stories in which a woman might respond to hearing that her husband is dead by thinking, "Now I'm going to get all that insurance money!" or "Now I'm free to marry the man I really love!" The woman singing "Supper Time" has to imagine what it would be like if she suddenly received news that someone she loved had been killed. This song will begin to come to life when the singer thinks, "I don't know how I'm going to go on living without him." That is, in fact, what the lyrics of the song actually tell us is this woman's response to the news of her husband's death.

> WW: Okay. You're upset because your girlfriend is mad at you.
>
> K: Yes.
>
> WW: Is she breaking up with you?
>
> K: I didn't think so.
>
> WW: Would you have a bigger problem if she did?
>
> K: Sure.
>
> WW: And what would that problem be?
>
> K: I got dumped!
>
> WW: And what was that like?
>
> K: I'm not sure.
>
> WW: Imagine it. Your girlfriend just broke up with you. Run that movie in your head.
>
> K: I'm hurt.
>
> WW: Good.
>
> K: I'm humiliated.
>
> WW: Even better. In fact, both "hurt" and "humiliated" are much better than "upset." You are hurt and humiliated. That's more immediate, right?
>
> K: Yes.
>
> WW: And much more powerful?
>
> K: Yes.
>
> WW: Why is it more powerful?

K: Because I feel like I want to do something about it.

WW: Good! Let's make your problem bigger still. What if she broke your engagement?

K: We're not engaged.

WW: You're the writer here. Would your story be better if you were engaged?

K: It would be more dramatic.

WW: Then if I were you, I would choose to have my girlfriend say to me that she no longer wants to be my wife and spend her life with me. Does that make your problem easier to envision—to experience?

K: Yeah.

WW: Great. Now...why is she breaking your engagement?

K: I...I have no idea.

WW: The words of the song say how much you love her. Right?

K: Now I'm just back where I started.

WW: Not really. But you are back at the fundamental nature of what the song is saying. What if she doesn't believe that you love her?

K: Why would she not believe me?

WW: Because you cheated on her.

K: I didn't cheat on her!

WW: We're just making this up.

K: But I don't like being a cheat. I wouldn't do that.

WW: Good. I'm glad to hear it. But "what if"? What if she thinks you are a cheat, and so she dumped you?

K: But that's not fair.

WW: Why not?

K: I didn't do it!

WW: You're being unjustly accused?

K: Right!

WW: In addition to already being hurt and humiliated? Is your problem getting bigger?

K: A lot bigger.

WW: Can you imagine yourself in a circumstance such as this?

K: I'm not sure I want to.

WW: But the actor in you does. This is just a game we're playing. The fact that in real life you and your girlfriend love and trust each other actually makes the game easier to play. And more fun.

K: Okay. So...if my girlfriend were to think I cheated on her it would be awful.

WW: And the more awful it is, the worse you will feel and the more likely you will be to do something about it. Right?

K: Right.

WW: So...what are you going to do?

K: I'm going to get her to take me back.

WW: How?

K: By singing "All the Things You Are" in a way that will make her know that I would never, ever cheat on her—not in a million years!

WW: And does that action feel big enough for such a big song?

K: Yes...finally!

WW: Great. You have a clearly articulated dramatic circumstance, and it is your discomfort in that circumstance—your problem—that will provide you with the fuel you need to sing the song.

Kevin's exploration of his circumstance and his search for his problem were based on what was actually his innate understanding of human nature. All he needed to do was imagine what it would be like to be in an increasingly dire situation. You have that ability as well. There are many things about human behavior, both your own and others', that you understand instinctively, regardless of your age or your life experience. You just have to take the time to imagine it. You have to play the game.

The Heart of Your "Problem"

As human beings we seek a consistent, if not constant, state of equilibrium. We instinctively try to maintain a state of physical, emotional, spiritual, and psychological balance. When we are out of balance in any way, we are not comfortable. If the imbalance increases, or continues for too long a time, we become so uncomfortable that we will take some specific action in an attempt to restore balance. The most effective way I have found to get to the heart of your problem is to look at your situation in the story you are devising by figuring out what is out of balance and why it is out of balance.

In order to do that, I find it is helpful to recognize that our fundamental sense of equilibrium is determined by how our needs are being met—or, more to the point, are not being met—in four essential areas.

We seek a state of *physical well-being*.

Physical well-being includes having enough to eat and drink, being protected from adverse conditions such as extreme heat or cold, and, of course, being in good health. Even though unaddressed physical needs are often the source of imbalance, actors have a tendency to discount the value of physical discomfort and the problems it creates. In life, physical discomfort will almost always outweigh any other kind of discomfort. If we take Kevin, our unjustly accused boyfriend, and put him outside his girlfriend's window in a rainstorm on a cold night, both his problem and his need to address that problem will take on an entirely new dimension.

We seek *love*.

Love is perhaps the most powerful emotion that provides fuel for our stories, and usually the kind of love that drives a story is a romantic love. Romantic love is for most people a major component of their sense of well-being, and a romantic love in peril is certainly at the heart of many a dramatic circumstance, both on and off the stage. The love we seek in order to keep ourselves in balance can certainly include romantic love, but we all need still another kind of love that can be just as important and just as compelling. Each of us has a fundamental need to see ourselves reflected positively in the eyes and the actions of the people around us. The words and deeds of our loved ones, whether they be lovers, family, or friends, tell us that we are cared for and respected. They tell us that we are visible. There are people who see us and know us. Our need for this kind of love, in all the various forms it may take, is primal. And loneliness, the lack of this kind of love, can be a powerful incentive for action.

We seek a means of *self-expression*.

It is not unusual for us to experience ourselves as unseen and unheard, and we very much need the world around us to see and hear us. We will, therefore, frequently seek the means to make ourselves more visible. We will find ways to get attention, to become larger and louder. Even if that is not possible or not in our nature, we will often find ways just to make sure we are noticed. We all try to speak in a "voice" that expresses who we are so clearly and effectively that anyone who encounters that voice will have no choice but to acknowledge it. In doing so, they validate our existence.

We seek the *material means* to provide for ourselves the things we need.

It is human nature to seek both security and power in our physical possessions, and we become anxious and fearful whenever we experience any significant lack of material means. No matter how psychologically or spiritually based our perspective on the first three essential components—the equilibrium we strive to achieve and maintain—there is no doubt that at certain points we are going to need some *stuff*. And stuff requires some system of barter. For most of us that means money. We need money to buy food to eat, clothes to keep us warm, and air conditioning to keep us cool. We need money to pay the doctor and buy medicine. We need money to buy the new car to impress the girlfriend, to pay for the classes to study art or music, and to provide the kind of financial security that will keep us and our loved ones safe from harm. A lack of money can drive anyone to desperation, and in addition to that, there are many stories told around a central character who has more than enough money but is still driven to get more.

Adjusting the Imbalance

Whenever your balance shifts, you will normally adjust instinctively and unconsciously. If you become uncomfortable in your chair and shift weight, it is unlikely that you think of that as an adjustment to an imbalance, even though that is exactly what it is. Through the course of your day, you make countless such adjustments of which you are not aware. Your mind and body carry out these functions without requiring that you pay attention.

There are other adjustments that you make more consciously but still without much difficulty or paying much attention. You get a drink of water when you are thirsty, or you get something to eat when you are hungry. You experience a call of nature and go to the bathroom. You make a joke to ease tension in a conversation. You reach out to a friend whom you feel you have neglected. You make a doctor's appointment because your cold is not getting better. In situations such as these you are aware of your behavior, and you know what your behavior is intended to accomplish. You do not usually think of these actions as an effort on your part to restore equilibrium, but if you think about these behaviors and observe them through the course of your day, you will realize that the restoration of equilibrium is exactly what these actions are meant to accomplish.

The degree of imbalance and the duration of the experience will determine how much you are actually aware that there is a problem. That awareness is what will inspire behavior and cause you to take an action.

Let's say you are hungry. How hungry you are is going to determine the kind of action that is required. You may go to the kitchen and make yourself some toast. You may go out to a restaurant and buy a sandwich. But if you have no food in the house and no money, and perhaps you have children who are hungry as well, you may go into a grocery store and steal a loaf of bread. While all of these actions are designed to address the same fundamental physical discomfort of being hungry, the size of the action will be determined both by the degree of the imbalance and by how many areas are out of balance at the same time. The person who steals the loaf of bread is addressing issues related to physical well-being, means, and love, and one could even make a pretty good case for self-expression.

Some imbalances, the ones that elicit the kind of behavior capable of bringing a dramatic circumstance to life, require that total attention be paid. In instances such as these, you will stop all other activity until you find a way to restore equilibrium. You may seek companionship to mitigate loneliness or seek protection when you are afraid. You might look for a job because you have no money or you might make a plan to steal some. You seek reconciliation because a relationship you care about is in trouble. You seek relief from pain, and you seek forgiveness for your "sins." These things are the true stuff of drama. They are the gold for which you are always mining.

It Is Not About Feelings

You can think of your problem in many different ways—imbalance, a state of discomfort, an aroused nervous system, discombobulation, an activated reptilian brain—as you can read about in chapter 14. However you choose to think about your problem or whatever you choose to call it, it is essential that you think of it as a physical sensation and not a state of emotion. You should never, for example, articulate your problem as either sadness or anger. These two particular states of emotion are especially attractive to actors, and they are a siren's song that can lure you to your destruction. I am going to address this in detail in the next chapter, but for now, suffice it to say that the problem with emotions is that they are not actually "actable." An emotion is something that happens, not something you seek.

I am aware that for many people my last statement opens up a proverbial can of worms. Even so, I think it bears repeating. An emotion is something that happens, not something you seek. There are many approaches to acting based on various means by which an actor can achieve an emotional state prior to actually beginning to act. The most famous of these would be the "Method," an approach to acting most often identified with Lee Strasberg and the Actors Studio. In his autobiography, *A Life* (Knopf, 1988), the legendary director Elia Kazan summed up his thoughts on the matter so succinctly that I will let his words address the issue.

> Increasingly it became evident in [Strasberg's] productions that the actors and actresses would perform on stage as if they were moving in a miasma of self-devotion....I, among others, turned against Lee's kind of instruction and sought simpler and more "present" methods of arousing emotions....The key was not the emotion, but what the character wanted to do, what his objective in the scene was. Precisely as in life.

Conversations about acting technique can inspire a lot of impassioned—even heated—talk, nearly as much as conversations about singing technique. Throughout my career as a director and teacher, I have always gravitated toward what worked. I am a pragmatist through and through, and while I believe that both practice and theory are essential to any description of any method of acting, it is practice that comes first and therefore practice that must inform the theory. I espouse the process I do because it works. I see it work every day in the classroom and onstage. And before I leave this chapter, I think it is a good idea to articulate the process one more time.

The problem that you are seeking to articulate and explore as part of your dramatic circumstance is a physical sense of discombobulation that you experience at the core of your being. You access that core by first working with a language that resonates within your own consciousness and then utilizing your breath and the centering process to connect that language to your mind and your body. The result will be behavior that is both emotionally grounded and truthful.

One student recently reported the following as she was working to combine two songs as part of a recital set: "The word that really resonated with me was *unsafe*. The idea of feeling *unsafe* inspired other thoughts such as insecure, vulnerable, and *reluctant*. But the word *unsafe* really gave me the visceral gut reaction that was lacking when I first sang the two songs."

Your effective exploration of any problem is dependent on how completely and willingly you commit to your "what if." In exploring the most dangerous and most compelling story you can tell, your imagination will allow you to experience your dramatic circumstance as something that belongs to you. That is the work that Kevin did in his coaching. He identified a problem and then progressed from a general state of unhappiness by creating a very specific circumstance. That circumstance then came to life through Kevin's willingness, coupled with an ability acquired through practice, to imagine what it would be like to be losing someone he loved because she believed that he had been unfaithful to her.

When you make a circumstance personal, you tap into your instincts, into your own life experience. That connection to your own experience and knowledge draws energy from your center, from the visceral part of yourself. And that visceral energy becomes the fuel for the actions you will be compelled to take in pursuit of the thing you must have.

10

Freeing Yourself from Obligation

In the previous chapter, you saw how Kevin explored and expanded the story at the heart of his dramatic circumstance in order to arrive at a problem that was big enough to fuel the song he was going to sing. By "big enough," I mean he found a problem that was both specific and personal. Kevin began his coaching thinking that the only action he could find in the words and music of his song was to tell his girlfriend that he loved her, but when he took the time to imagine various scenarios that might occur in and around a romantic relationship, he ended up with an action that required him to do everything in his power to save that relationship from coming to a terrible end. Thus, the behavior his story inspired was much more interesting and compelling, not only for the people watching Kevin perform, but for Kevin himself.

The work that Kevin did was a perfect example of what is often referred to as "raising the stakes." It is a phrase you hear a lot in acting classes, but it is one that I avoid. I find that for most people, the mental image of what it means to raise the stakes too easily leads to energy being generated for the sake of energy itself, and everything just gets louder and faster. Any application of generalized energy, which I sometimes refer to as "stepping on the gas," encourages an actor to push—or specifically, to create a level of extraneous physical tension in order to ensure that there is something to push against.

How can words alone lead to pushing? Words, based on how they have been used in your past, have connections to both the conscious and subconscious parts of your brain. They have meanings that have grown out of your personal experience. Thus, the words you choose will create both physical and emotional connections to the story you are telling, and they can propel you into certain responses and behaviors without you even being aware that they are doing so. This is sometimes helpful and sometimes not. The power of language is certainly a benefit to you as an actor. Language is the very foundation of the work you are doing, and when it is employed imaginatively and productively, it is without a doubt your most valuable tool. However, there is a downside to the power of language. Words can just as easily hinder the work you are trying to do if the words you choose turn into *obligations*.

The obligation trap is something that all actors fall victim to at some time or another, to some degree or another, and oddly enough, falling into that trap is usually the result of how hard the actor is working. Whenever actors fall into this trap, they end up expending a lot of well-intentioned energy in a totally unproductive way. The obligation trap is something you want to be able to recognize and avoid.

What exactly are obligations? Obligations are decisions you make that you should sound a certain way, or look a certain way, or—in taking on the most constrictive and destructive "should" of all—feel a certain way. Please keep in mind that, in this context of constrictive "shoulds," I am using the word *feel* to refer to feeling a particular emotion or set of emotions. I am not referring to feeling the physical sensations of breath, resonance, or airflow that are essential to a singer's work. When a particular "should" becomes attached to a song, it manifests itself as an obligation. Thus an obligation becomes a responsibility, of which the performer is always conscious, to achieve a particular result. Obligations pull you out of your process and ask that you monitor results.

As a performer, you are often asked to produce a specific set of results. Those results tend to involve the replication of either the sounds some other singer has made or the work some other actor has done while performing that same material. Whether or not you are successful in *your* work is then determined by how effectively you are able to replicate the work that someone else has already done. That is not making art, and that is not making music.

The problem with result-oriented thinking is twofold. First of all, you must meet the expectations of other people who are setting the standard for what you are going to do. Second of all, and what becomes more problematic, is that you must meet your own standards and your own expectation of results. You start out with an idea of what your performance is supposed to look like or sound like, and then you work very hard to make sure that is the thing you achieve. And the only way you can figure out if you are achieving those results is to listen to yourself and watch yourself. That is the antithesis of what you want to be doing.

How do you avoid listening to yourself and watching yourself? You focus on a process that allows you to stop constantly monitoring how you are doing because you are too busy *actually doing something*. When you are living fully inside a dramatic circumstance, you have no choice but to monitor how your other is doing, because you have identified an other who is the key to accomplishing your objective. Your mother is going to rescue you. Your girlfriend is going to agree to marry you. Your brave self is going to give you the strength to take action.

Result-oriented work kills both creativity and discovery, and a result-oriented mindset is unfortunately all too common in young performers. It is also, and even more unfortunately, all too common in people who teach young performers. Obligations may be handed to you by a teacher, or demanded by a director, or, as we are taught to believe, required by the character or the text. Most obligations, however, we happily take on ourselves. We make assumptions about certain kinds of people, certain classes of people, and certain periods of history. We decide that particular emotions must be attached to particular dramatic situations, and we set out to make sure that we either reach that emotional state or, more problematically, appear to have reached that emotional state. We decide where we are supposed to go rather than taking the journey that will allow us to discover where we can go. Obligations become filters through which our natural impulses must be processed, and the result of that filtering is that our natural impulses are either obscured or, as is more often and most sadly the case, lost altogether.

Obligations get in the way of your ability to discover what something can be. More significantly, they get in the way of discovering who you can be.

Divide and Conquer

The first step in identifying and eliminating an obligation is to figure out just where it comes from. Once you locate the source of obligatory thinking, you will be better able to change that thinking and rid yourself of that particular obligation, while at the same time ridding yourself of the distraction that comes with it. I find it helpful to break obligations into three distinct categories: behavioral, technical, and emotional.

Behavioral Obligations

A behavioral obligation is usually the result of misinterpreted, or misapplied, information that comes from either a script or the research an actor may have done in regard to a specific character or a specific time in history. These are the obligations that cause an actor to say, "I now have to behave in this manner because the script dictates that I behave in this manner." You can substitute the word *character* or *style* for the word *script* in that statement, and you will end up with the same problem. We are going to look more closely at behavioral obligations later in this chapter.

Technical Obligations

The source of technical obligations is the misapplication—or, more often, the mistiming—of a performer's singing technique or acting technique. If you can only approach a certain passage of music by thinking about whether or not your air is moving in a way that will allow you easy access to the high note, then you are not ready to perform that piece of music. If you cannot sing a particular song without constantly checking to see if everything is in proper working order, you are not ready to perform that song. A very perceptive voice teacher once said to a student in a performance class she was observing, "No one is interested in watching you give yourself a voice lesson." In order to address technical obligations, you must learn to differentiate between what is practice and what is performance. When it comes time to perform, it is your job to prepare yourself in such a way as to assure that your technique will function at its optimum level. Having completed that preparation, you must then trust your technique and get on with the job of achieving your objective.

Emotional Obligations

Emotional obligations come about as the result of an actor's expectation of what a character is supposed to be feeling because of the things that are happening to that character in that particular circumstance. To my way of thinking, emotional obligations are the most crippling of them all. Discovering what a character might feel as he or she grapples with the circumstance in which he or she is living—and allowing yourself to experience that feeling—is immediate and dramatic and a very exciting proposition. Deciding what a character is supposed to be feeling is the quickest way to drain the life out of your work. Emotional obligations have a tendency to attach themselves to technical obligations, and vice versa. The music seems to dictate a certain feeling, so you decide that you must express that feeling in both your demeanor and the sound of your voice. When you begin your work by deciding what you are supposed to be feeling, you are likely to get yourself in big trouble in a big hurry. It is never your job to express feelings. It is your job to take real, committed, actual do-something actions in pursuit of the thing you want. It is in taking actions that your feelings will be revealed, to you as well as to your audience.

I generally find that musicians are disciplined in their habits and conscientious in their work ethic. They tend to be, or have always been, very good students, and I imagine you are no exception. It is a good thing if you are disciplined and hardworking and take your work seriously. It is a not-so-good thing if the "good student" in you is all too willing to join forces with the part of you that wants so very much to succeed. Together these two perfectionist identities speak in a powerful, usually loud, voice, which cajoles and bullies you into shouldering a very long list of "shoulds."

Connecting to Your Emotions

There is no question that audiences want to see and hear performers who are making emotional connections to the words they speak and sing. All of us who work in the theatre want to find an emotional connection to what we are doing, and I am sure that you want to work with a process that will evoke emotional connections that are both consistent and truthful. Unfortunately, the desire for an emotional connection leads many actors to pursue their feelings rather than pursue their objectives, and the pursuit of feelings is truly a no-win proposition, for performer and audience alike.

Acting is about behavior, and the study of acting is about the exploration of possible behaviors. You must be able and willing to investigate anything and everything that you might conceivably do in order to satisfy your objective. The key to finding an emotional connection in your work is in the commitment you make to your objective—your on-the-spot-what-you-are-doing-right-this-moment objective. It is often the case that a wholehearted commitment to your actions will propel you to a place where what you are feeling will be revealed. It is, however, of critical importance that you make the distinction between *expressing feelings* and *revealing feelings*.

Expressing your feelings is a fruitless pursuit of something that is actually contrary to human nature. Revealing your feelings is a phenomenon of human behavior that is grounded in the way human beings actually behave. Revealing your feelings is something that happens rather than something that you do, and because such revelation is common to all human beings, as well as consistent with everyone's experience of normal human behavior, your audience will perceive the revelation as truthful.

Let's look at a specific coaching where the singer needed to make a clear distinction between what is a problem and what is an emotional obligation. Melanie is working on her dramatic circumstance for the George and Ira Gershwin song "But Not for Me," in which she tells us that everyone but her seems to be finding true love. She sang the song, and I turned to the other students in the class.

WW: Based on what we just saw and heard, what do we know about the person singing the words "They're writing songs of love, but not for me"?

St#1: That she has a good voice.

WW: That's certainly true. Melanie has a lovely voice. What else do we know?

St#2: That she's sad.

WW: And why do we know that?

St#3: Because she looks sad. She sounds sad.

WW: Okay. So we know that Melanie has a good voice, and that she is apparently sad. Do we know anything else?

Nobody said anything, because there really wasn't anything to say.

In any song you sing, you want the people watching and hearing you to get a sense of who you are and what it would be like to be in your situation. That is the power of singing and the very thing that draws people to songs in the first place. Songs give us a look inside a person's heart and soul. Audiences do want to hear good voices, but good voices, in the world of both professional and amateur singing, are not all that hard to find. What an audience wants most of all is to hear and see someone who in their singing and acting sheds light on what it is to be human. The way to accomplish that is to get inside your circumstance and behave as if the dramatic events you imagine were actually happening to you in that very moment.

WW: So, Melanie... were you sad?

M: Well... I was trying to be.

WW: Why were you trying to be sad?

M: Because I thought that's what I would be in this circumstance.

WW: You decided that the person singing this song needed to be sad.

M: Yes.

WW: But you were not experiencing any actual sadness, right?

M: Right.

WW: And so you were pretending to be sad?

M: Well... I guess you'd have to say that.

WW: And what did that feel like?

M: Fake.

WW: Right. If the first thing we decide about a song is that the person singing it is sad, one of two things is going to happen. You will either fail in your effort to actually be sad, or you will be forced to pretend. And in this case, pretending is just another word for lying.

M: That sounds bad.

WW: It's not the kind of work we set out to do.

M: I agree.

WW: And it's not any fun.

M: I totally agree with that!

Melanie was certainly not the first singer, nor will she be the last, to fall victim to this kind of thinking. We decide that a certain feeling is required, and then we take on an obligation to appear as if we are feeling that feeling. Both consciously and unconsciously, we dutifully filter everything through that obligation. Your audience may well know that you are sad, but more likely they will know that they are supposed to believe you are sad. Either way, a general quality of sadness is the only information they are getting from you, and it is a good bet that neither you nor your audience are having a very good time.

WW: What made you decide you were sad?

M: Well, I'm in love with this boy who doesn't seem to be in love with me. He's left town without even saying goodbye.

WW: And does the word *sad* describe what you are experiencing?

M: No...not really.

WW: Why not?

M: It's not enough.

WW: Right. "Sad" is an insufficient response to what has happened to you, and it is an obligation that is getting in your way. You've described feelings that you are going to have to pretend to have because you don't actually have those feelings for this imagined other. Nothing you've

said is inaccurate or untrue, but you have not
reached the point where you have something
that requires you to take an action.

If you take a minute to think about it, you will realize that
sadness is not actually the way we respond to loss, particularly in
the immediate aftermath of a loss. Sadness, or even depression,
may set in later, but as problematic as sadness and depression may
be, neither is dramatic. Neither requires that you take an action.

I asked Melanie to take some time to think, "What if someone I
loved were to abandon me?" I asked her to breathe and center and
then try to see that movie in her head. After a few minutes, it was
obvious by the expression on her face that Melanie was occupying
her circumstance in a different way.

WW: What's your problem now?

M: My heart is breaking.

WW: That's better. And what does a person do when
her heart is breaking?

M: She tries to fix it.

WW: That's right! If your heart is breaking, it is only
logical that you will be trying to find some way
to fix it. At the very least you will be trying to
minimize the pain.

M: How would I do that?

WW: You tell me.

M: Well, I guess I could turn to someone for
help.

WW: What would you want that someone to do?

M: To know how I feel.

WW: And then do what?

M: That's what is so hard! What can I do? What can anyone actually do?

WW: You can ask for help.

M: Is that enough?

WW: It's a lot.

M: But it's not going to work. You can't really mend a broken heart.

WW: That's right. But you can try, and that is something worth doing and worth watching. Lots of times the best songs and the most powerful dramatic circumstances are failed attempts to fix something that is not, in reality, fixable. It's the struggle that empowers you, and it's the struggle that an audience cares about. Struggling with life's problems is what they identify with. We don't need to see you win, but we do need to see you try.

M: May I do it again?

WW: Of course. Who are you going to sing to?

M: I'm going to sing to my best friend.

WW: Why her?

M: Because she never really liked the guy in the first place, and she is telling me that I'm better off without him and that she can't understand why I'm so upset.

WW: Good choices. What do you want her to do?

M: I want her to be my friend and give me her support rather than her criticism.

WW: Excellent. Let's add one more dimension to your problem. Do you actually want to tell her these things?

M: Yes.

WW: You do?

M: Well, I want her to help me feel better.

WW: And what's the price you're going to have to pay for that?

M: I have to reveal things that are really hard to say.

WW: Exactly. You have to admit to her that it feels as if no one has ever loved you and no one is ever going to. That's not something we admit lightly. It's not something we want to say out loud. Maybe the woman who suddenly finds herself in this position has never said these words out loud before.

M: That changes my problem.

WW: How?

M: I not only have a broken heart but I have to admit some things about my life that I don't want to admit.

WW: And this starts to get very interesting. Now, take your time. Breathe and center, and let's see what happens.

Melanie began to sing the song again. About three-quarters of the way through the first line, she suddenly choked up. She kept trying to get the words out but was not actually able to make any sound without crying. She struggled through to the end of the song and barely managed to get out the last four words: "he's not for me."

M: What do I do about that?!

WW: About what?

M: I can't perform the song if I can't actually sing.

WW: You're not ready to perform the song. The song is in process.

M: What do I do?

WW: You sing it again and again and again. You put yourself in the same situation and you work to make your friend understand what is happening to you. And over time, probably a matter of weeks, your need to get the words out will be more powerful than the despair that is now overwhelming you. You will absolutely reach the point where you are able to sing the song, but at the same time you will always know what it is costing you.

I again turned to students in the class for their reaction to Melanie's work.

St#2: I knew even before she started singing that there was something wrong.

WW: What do you mean?

St#2: She was trying to stay calm and focused. Trying to breathe.

WW: What did that tell you?

St#2: That she was dealing with something powerful.

WW: What else?

St#1: I believe that she really loved the guy.

WW: Why is that?

St#1: Because her behavior seemed more honest. It looked like she was telling the truth. It looked like she didn't want to be there, but she had to be.

The steps that Melanie took in this coaching were significant. She moved away from thinking of her problem as a feeling, and she gave up the obligation of being sad because the love of her life had abandoned her. Instead she placed herself in a very uncomfortable circumstance that required immediate action. These changes in her thinking will have a profound impact on the way Melanie sings this song, because she is now able to live inside a story that is much more honest and much more powerful. And whenever she sings this song, her audience will recognize that she is sharing with them an experience that is actually costing her something and that, therefore, resonates with them as being true.

The "V" Word

This is usually the point in every class when someone starts talking about vulnerability, both a word and a state of being that I find actors to be inordinately fond of. As a director and a teacher, I am fond of it myself. However, it is important that we recognize vulnerability as a product of behavior and not a state of being that we are trying to achieve. The dictionary definition of the word *vulnerable* is "susceptible to physical or emotional attack or harm." You are susceptible when you are not adequately defended.

Because Melanie was willing to tell her friend the absolute truth, and because she had no choice but to accept whatever her friend's response might be, she was susceptible to her friend's reaction. That made Melanie vulnerable, but the important thing to keep in mind is that Melanie's vulnerability was not a *feeling*. It was a state of being that came about as a result of her behavior.

No rational person would ever choose vulnerability as a state of being. As rational people, we spend a lot of time figuring out just how best to protect ourselves. We do this both consciously and unconsciously. We give up those protections only when we want something so much that the getting of it requires that we reveal ourselves. Only then are we willing to be "naked"—and even then, not for very long.

As an actor, you will be asked to live in the dramatic context of any number of life circumstances in which people may find themselves, and as you imagine yourself in these circumstances, you will see that the actions people take in dramatic situations are almost always fueled by need and almost never fueled by feelings.

Don't our needs and our feelings have an impact on each other? Of course they do. But as an actor you are well advised to focus on your needs, because it is need that inspires action. Let your feelings take care of themselves.

The Nature of Feelings

Human beings are generally uncomfortable in any heightened emotional state, regardless of what that state might be. We do not like the sensation of losing control, and that is true even in instances where the feelings to which we might surrender are feelings that we would classify as good feelings. I can think of several examples:

- People who are brought to tears by a given situation are almost always trying not to cry—trying not to display the emotions they are feeling.
- People who receive sudden good news are usually reluctant to express joy until being totally reassured that the news is real—that unbelievable good fortune is actually theirs.

- People confronted with news of tragedy will most often try to silence the source of the news, hoping that what they are hearing will turn out not to be true.
- People who are overwhelmed by feelings of love can come up with as many reasons to hide and protect those feelings as they can to express them.

The reason that people in these situations try to suppress what they are feeling is their fear that their feelings are going to interfere with their actual ability to function. They are afraid that their feelings will prevent them from saying what they need to say or doing what they need to do. That is in fact what happened to Melanie when she committed to an action and suddenly found herself crying.

It is only human nature for you to try to control your feelings in order to remain clear-headed and focused, and when confronted with an emotionally charged situation, the natural human response is for you to try to keep your feelings at bay. That is the truest human response and one we recognize when we see it happening in other people. Oftentimes, however, your emotions will not be kept at bay. They reach the point, just as they did for Melanie when admitting her real fear to her friend, where they simply overpower you. It is important to keep in mind that Melanie's feelings were not encouraged to surface, asked to surface, or even allowed to surface. They, in fact, overcame her resistance to letting them surface. It was against her will that her feelings were revealed. This can be a difficult concept to grasp, but I believe that practice will teach you that the action of trying to keep your feelings under control is what will most often cause them to emerge.

When you approach any piece of dramatic material, you have to remember to ask yourself, "What do I need to do?" not "What do

I need to feel?" And you really have to remember not to ask yourself, "What am I *supposed* to feel?"

What do you do instead? You commit yourself body and soul to the action that is demanded by the circumstance in which you have imagined yourself to be.

The Tyranny of "Character"

When you consider the coachings we have reviewed thus far, you will realize that what they all have in common is my desire for the singers to make each story their own story. That is, I believe, the key to their most powerful work.

But what about creating a "character"? In my opinion, the importance of "character" is overstated, and the word is overused. I find so often that it is the way actors think about "character" that saddles them with a set of obligations that get in the way of the work. Their obligation to character leads them to behavior that does not make sense, or keeps them from following their own impulses. I have directed *The Sound of Music* many times, and it is par for the course that when we reach that point in rehearsal when Maria confronts the Captain about his neglect of his children, I have a conversation with the actress playing Maria that goes something like this:

> M: I don't think she would raise her voice to the
>   Captain.
> WW: Why not?
> M: Well, she's been raised by nuns. She's a good
>   girl. She's considerate and polite.
> WW: Are you considerate and polite?
> M: Yes. I think so.

WW: Do you have a child in your life of whom you are particularly fond?

M: My sister's little boy. He's four.

WW: What's he like?

M: Oh my goodness, he's adorable! He's really smart and has the oddest sense of humor. He just makes me laugh.

WW: So if someone were being mean to him...if someone were hurting his feelings, what would you do?

M: I'd stop them.

WW: You'd protect him.

M: Of course.

WW: How?

M: However I had to.

WW: Would you raise your voice?

M: At least that!

WW: Right. And that's what Maria is doing. She is protecting the children she has come to love from the person who is hurting them. That is why the scene is so powerful, why it's a turning point in the story, why the Captain is so taken aback that he actually fires her. You and Maria have one job, and it's the same job—to take care of those children. You don't need to spend one second taking care of the character of Maria or worrying about what she would or would not do.

In my experience most actors are one-hundred-percent committed to "finding the character." I know this sounds like a perfectly acceptable thing for an actor to do. The problem, however, with this view of acting is the fact that the characters who inhabit plays and books and movies do not actually exist. Remember the David Mamet quote from chapter 4.

> There is no character. There are only lines upon a page. They are lines of dialogue meant to be said by the actor. When he or she says them simply, in an attempt to achieve an object more or less like that suggested by the author, the audience sees an illusion of a character upon the stage.

Characters come to life through their behavior. That behavior consists of what the character does and says, and those things are determined by the writer. So it is not, in my opinion, an actor's job to find the character. The character does not need to be found. It is also not the actor's job to "become" the character. That is impossible. It is the actor's job to speak the words and take the actions provided by the writer and to do that as if he or she were actually in that circumstance. The question that actor must ask is not "What would my character do?" The question is "In what kind of circumstance would I say and do these things that this character is saying and doing?" The actress playing Maria is going to do everything she can to protect the seven Von Trapp children from their father. But she is not going to do that because of what she knows about Maria. She's going to do it because of what she knows about herself.

Doesn't that mean that you are always then playing yourself? The simple answer to that question is "Yes. You are always playing yourself." A more nuanced answer, and a more enlightened one, is that in the process of exploring and learning a role, you discover aspects of yourself and your own nature that would compel you to speak the same words and take the same actions as the character you are playing. Furthermore, you must be willing to reveal those aspects of yourself and your own nature. You don't have to have had a child in order to explore the circumstances in which you would behave as a parent. You do not have to have killed someone in order to imagine yourself in such a dire situation that murder becomes your only option.

One of my favorite actresses of all time is Judi Dench. I have seen her both on stage and, of course, in movies and on television, and in every character she plays, the essential essence of Judi Dench is always present. From what appears to be a place of extraordinary self-knowledge, coupled with her obvious delight in exploring a wide range of human behaviors, Dame Judi has successfully played everything from Cleopatra to Queen Elizabeth I to the head of the British Secret Service to a repressed lesbian schoolteacher whose obsessions and denial of those obsessions are driving her to madness. Judi Dench has not brought these people and their stories to life by committing to "character." She has accomplished this by committing to *behavior*.

Characters are defined by what you say or do, not by what you think or feel. It is the script that tells you what your character is going to say and do, and it's your job to say and do those things as if you were in the same circumstance as your character. You are encouraged, and rightly so, to read scripts and analyze the characters you are going to play. It is consequently easy to assume that because you know the story of the play and the biography of the character, including all the various details on which you might be tested, you have completed the work you need to prepare yourself to play the role. For the kind of work we are doing here, that is not the case.

Significant information may indeed come from a script, but the most powerful decisions will come from you. Referring back to Katerina's work on "Where Is Love?," it was not her job to try to "become" Oliver. It was not even her job to try to figure out Oliver. It was her job to imagine what it would be like to be in the same situation as that lost and lonely little boy, and she did that by asking herself, "What if I were alone, unloved, cold, hungry, and locked up?"

It is all too easy, particularly for those of us who spend a lot of time in schools and universities, to bring a classroom mentality to the acting process. The good student presumes that there is a right answer, which means that the good student must find that right answer in order to give it back to the teacher and get a good grade. This kind of thinking will not only get in the way of your creativity, but it will also prevent you from discovering the power of your own ideas and your own impulses.

It is true that your success in bringing a character "off the page" is dependent on your ability to draw relevant information from the text with which you are working. However, the relevant information you are seeking is what that character is actually doing. It is your ability to inform your character's behavior with your own imagination and your own life experience that will truly bring each character to life, and when you are able to commit to behavior in a truthful way, the audience will absolutely believe in the character you are portraying. At the same time, you will be able to believe in yourself as you commit to the behavior of the character you are playing, and you will be fully present in the scenes you are playing. You will come to life and reveal yourself through the character that you are portraying.

In the final analysis, is it you or is it the character? The answer is that it does not really matter, and your audience will not even know that there is any difference.

What Might Happen

Obligations make it much harder, if not impossible, for you to immerse yourself in a process whereby you can find your own voice, your own impulses, your own actions, and yes, even your own feelings. If you work with a teacher or director who shows you how to commit to a process that allows you to discover what something might be rather than what it is supposed to be, you will be able to stop worrying about the acceptability of the outcome of your work. I assure you that the work that you do mindfully and truthfully will always be acceptable. But more than acceptable, it will be yours. It will be uniquely and truly yours.

How often do you ask your teacher or your director, "Does what I am doing look and sound like it is supposed to look and sound?" We seldom put the question in those exact words, but we do ask it all the time.

Let me ask you some different kinds of questions. What might happen if your measure of success were determined by your level of commitment to a process rather than the achievement of some predetermined outcome? What might happen if you had a specific set of steps to follow and a vocabulary to describe those steps that was practical, proactive, positive, and achievable?

I think that you might experience a sense of actual accomplishment, and with that accomplishment, you might begin to feel a sense of freedom in your work. You might feel that you were in charge of the work you were doing. You might reward yourself for work well done and then challenge yourself to follow those same steps again—and in doing so, you might discover that your sense of freedom only gets greater and your work gets even better.

Commit to a process and learn how to evaluate your work in terms of the steps that you are taking as part of that process. Let the results take care of themselves. Trust me. They will.

11

Choosing an Other

In the late 1990s, the playwright David Hare was performing his one-man play *Via Dolorosa* on Broadway at the same time Judi Dench was performing on Broadway in Hare's play *Amy's View*. (For her performance in *Amy's View*, Judi Dench won the 1999 Tony Award for Best Performance by a Leading Actress in a Play.) As he recounts in *Acting Up* (Faber & Faber, 1999), Hare, who was struggling with the challenges of performing by himself eight times a week, asked Judi Dench if she had ever done a "one-man" show. She told him that she was offered them all the time but always turned them down. "I couldn't do them," she said. "When I was getting ready I wouldn't know who I was getting ready for. I have to believe I'm going down there to meet someone." That is who your *other* needs to be: the "someone" you are "going down there to meet."

In the world of music theatre and opera, singers are constantly asked to perform in their own "one-man" shows, because that is essentially what it means to stand up and sing a solo. And in those instances, it is imperative that you provide for yourself the "someone" that you are going "down there" to meet. You have to have someone to sing to, and you have to figure out just who that is going to be.

The solo song plays a pivotal role in both your training as a singer and your professional life. It is with a solo that you are expected to demonstrate your ability to sing and your ability to act, and like it or not, it is usually your performance of a solo song that is going to determine whether or not you will be called back or cast in a production, win a place in a school or apprentice program, or be deemed to have given a successful performance. That is a lot of weight to put on one piece of material.

Acting teachers will often ask you to think of solo songs as monologues, and we generally accept the fact that solo songs are monologues because we know that the singer of the song is so often alone on stage. And there is no doubt that you are alone when singing a song in an audition. The characterization, however, of a solo song as a monologue can lead you astray, and I ask you to consider that no one engages in an act of communication without some expectation of being responded to by someone who hears what is being communicated. I believe that statement holds true both onstage and off, and it is even more true when a dramatic circumstance dictates that you are literally separated from the person to whom you are singing, be that person a lost or distant love, a faraway friend, or an unresponsive God.

Thus, there are two guiding principles I want you to keep in mind when approaching a solo song. First, you must always look at a monologue, whether spoken or sung, as a scene that is taking place between you and another person. Second, you must search your dramatic circumstance for the most powerful *other* you can find.

An Array of Choices

Let's consider how you might go about choosing the most effective other for any song you are going to sing. In order to do that, we are going to take a look at another coaching in which the problem is a broken heart. There are lots of "broken heart" songs out there just waiting to be sung, and one of the best ways to avoid the "sadness obligation," such as we saw Melanie falling victim to when she began her work on "But Not for Me," is to figure out exactly to whom your song is being sung.

The singer in this coaching is Joanne, and the song is "Autumn" from the Richard Maltby and David Shire revue *Starting Here, Starting Now*. In this song, a woman tells us that she feels forever trapped in an endless autumn because that is when the love of her life walked out the door.

WW: So, Joanne, we've established that your problem is that you have a broken heart. Who is going to fix that for you?

J: That's who I'm going to sing to, right?

WW: Right. The person who can fix your broken heart is going to be your other.

J: Well…there are lots of choices.

WW: I agree. Let's talk about those.

J: I could be singing to myself.

WW: You could. In fact, for a song like this it may well end up that singing to yourself is the most logical choice. But I'd like to save that option and explore it a little later. For now I want you to pick someone to sing to—an other who can help you mend your broken heart.

J: My best friend?

WW: Why your best friend?

J: Because she always listens to me and supports me.

WW: So all you have to do is report to her what is going on?

J: That doesn't sound very dramatic.

WW: It isn't. Sharing your thoughts and feelings with an attentive and supportive friend is never going to be dramatic. It's just reporting information to a receptive other, and there is no conflict. Unless, of course, your friend views your circumstance differently than you do and is willing to tell you so.

J: Er...probably not.

WW: Let's try something. I want you to sing the song again, and this time I want you to sing it to me.

J: To you?

WW: I'm your wish-granting other. I have the power to give you the thing that you want, and you're going to have to use your words in order to get me to do that.

J: Okay.

WW: Take the time you need to breathe and center. Focus right on me.

Joanne sang the song keeping her focus on me for the entire time.

WW: So, how was that?

J: Intense.

WW: Intense how?

J: I couldn't really think about anything except what you were going to do.

WW: And what was I going to do?

J: That's just it. I had no idea if you were going to give me what I wanted, so I had to keep thinking of what I was going to do next that might win you over.

WW: And what was that experience like?

J: Really...it's hard to describe. It was strange. It kind of consumed me. I couldn't think about anything else.

WW: And is that a good thing?

J: Well, I certainly wasn't worried about my singing.

I asked students to give us some feedback.

WW: Did anyone notice anything?

St#3: Her voice. It seemed stronger and clearer.

WW: I agree. And why was that?

St#3: Probably because she wasn't really thinking about it.

WW: So did her vocal technique and all her training go away?

St#3: No. It just worked.

WW: And that's the goal—for you to allow your technique to work for you when you need it to.

The dramatic circumstance process is not about vocal technique. The process will, however, inform your technique and help you learn to trust it. When you organize your thoughts and prepare in a way that allows you to live more immediately in a dramatic circumstance, you are likely to find the experience liberating at every level, including vocally.

WW: So, Joanne, how are you going to recreate this experience?

J: Have you standing there every time I sing this song.

WW: Actually, that is exactly what you need to do. You need to have a powerful other standing in front of you who is going to decide your fate. And what will that force you to do?

J: It will force me to focus on what my other is actually doing.

WW: Exactly! That's the test of your action. You want me to grant your wish, and until it is granted you cannot stop working. What was the most immediate thing you experienced when you were singing to me?

J: That you were probably not going to help me.

WW: And why is that?

J: You didn't seem to understand what I was feeling.

WW: Or care.

J: Right.

WW: So it became your job to get me to care. To get my attention. To figure out what I'm thinking and see what kind of language makes me listen to you more carefully, or considerately. When you sang to me you were singing to an other who was going to make you work hard to get the thing you wanted. Right?

J: Right.

WW: How did you know that?

J: Well, I know you.

WW: Right. The fact that you need to work hard and concentrate is the nature of our relationship as student and teacher. What else?

J: You were standing right there in front of me.

WW: And that's the key to finding an other who is going to make you work your hardest to get the thing you want. It's someone you know who is standing right there in front of you.

When Joanne was singing to me she did not have to spend any time figuring out who I was or how she felt about me. Our relationship already existed. She just needed to figure out how to get me to do what she wanted me to do. Your work on a song must include the creation of an other with whom you have a relationship.

This is why working with an "as if" can be very helpful. An "as if" allows you to work with an other whom you know and to whom you are likely to respond without having to give it much thought. An "as if" is not meant to evoke feelings. It is meant to provide you with a relationship. If a scene requires you to try to convince a friend to get help with a drinking problem, you might choose to approach your friend "as if" you were talking to your brother. This allows you to invest immediately in your task because you already understand the relationship. The others that you create must become as real to you as people you actually know.

WW: Who can you sing to who views your situation differently than you do?

J: My mom.

WW: Why your mom?

J: Well...I do trust her and I think she could help me. Is that okay?

WW: There's nothing wrong with that, as long as she isn't going to just agree with everything you say.

J: She never does that.

WW: Good, at least for the purposes of your song circumstance.

J: I can see my mother not taking me seriously.

WW: Why not?

J: Because she thinks that I always make bad decisions.

WW: And if she thinks that, and she is your other, what is likely to happen?

J: She'll have a hard time supporting me because she never liked him in the first place. She thought he was a bad choice.

WW: So what does that choice do to your circumstance?

J: It makes my problem bigger.

WW: How's that?

J: It creates another level of insecurity.

WW: And is that a good thing?

J: Well...a bigger problem gives me more to work with.

WW: Bingo! You chose an other, and you identified what it is about that other that would make it harder to sing to her. That has enriched your problem. Tell me again what your problem is.

J: I have been left by a man I desperately love, and I feel abandoned and betrayed.

WW: And adding your mother to the mix...?

J: I'm abandoned, betrayed, and not respected in the choices I have made for my life.

WW: And the fun never stops! As you work with any of the elements of your dramatic circumstance, the choices you make will have an impact on the other elements. Allowing the elements of your circumstance to evolve in this way is a good thing, a very good thing. So…what does "not respected" by your mother feel like?

J: Uh…like she doesn't know who I really am.

WW: Like she doesn't really see you—see who you really are?

J: Right. Or hear me.

WW: Good. So if you articulate your problem as not being seen and not being heard, what does that do for your objective?

J: I need to get her to see me and hear me.

WW: Exactly. A more specific other leads to a more specific problem, which leads to a more specific objective. You want her to see you and hear you. And then what do you want her to do?

J: There's more?

WW: Well, why did you go to your mother in the first place?

J: Because she can be really supportive sometimes.

WW: When are those times?

J: [*laughing*] When I get her to see me and hear me.

WW: Then what does she do?

J: She offers me reassurance. Tells me everything is going to be okay.

WW: Great. So she can be a difficult other, but she's worth the effort.

J: Yeah.

WW: Let's play some more. What if you were singing to your father?

J: Oh, that would be really difficult.

WW: Why?

J: Because he doesn't see me as a grown-up and doesn't *want* me to be one. He would hate the idea that I was actually living with a guy.

WW: A guy to whom you weren't married?

J: Married or not. He would hate it.

WW: So he would be less likely to help you.

J: He wouldn't even want to talk about it in the first place.

WW: So, given that he is so resistant, can you think of any reason why you would go to him for help?

J: He's really smart. He might have some helpful answers to my problem.

WW: Would getting those answers be harder than getting comfort from your mom?

J: A lot harder.

WW: And it would require behavior that is braver, and more focused.

J: Would that be right for this song?

WW: It could be, but we're not really worried about "right." You want to be creative, to explore possibilities. You will discover along the way what feels best for you, and what's best will be whatever interests you and excites you the most, because that is what will pull you more completely into your story. For dramatic circumstances, replace the word *right* with *potent*.

J: Got it.

WW: To whom else could you be singing?

J: Well...I guess I could be singing to the guy.

WW: And what would that circumstance be?

J: I ran into him about eight months after he broke up with me, and it's kind of awkward, and he asks me how I'm doing.

WW: And why would you tell him?

J: Because I want to be honest.

WW: Do you really want to be *that* honest?

J: Maybe not.

WW: But can you imagine any circumstance in which you might actually say these things to the guy who left you?

J: It could be that he catches me at a really bad time when I don't have the strength to protect myself.

WW: That's good.

J: But that's really scary!

WW: Why's that?

J: Because I'm going to reveal the fact that his leaving me really broke my heart and that I'm still not over it.

WW: And why would you do something like that?

J: Because I don't feel as if I have any other choice. I don't have the strength to pretend that I'm not really messed up.

WW: And once you reveal yourself in this way, what can he do?

J: He can either stay with me...or leave again.

WW: He can return your feelings.

J: Or not.

WW: That *is* scary. And this choice puts you at the greatest risk we've found so far.

J: So does that make it the best choice?

WW: That's up to you to decide. It certainly makes it the most fun choice.

J: Fun?!

WW: It is a story. It is a song. It is not real life. You are in the process of figuring out how to occupy your circumstance, how to live inside this particular story that you want to tell. The more difficult the circumstance, the more you will be compelled to act, and the more interesting your work is going to be. Both for you doing it and for the people who are watching you do it.

Joanne is exploring choices that make her task more demanding and that will consequently make her actions more clear. With each other she considers, her problem changes to some degree, which means that her objective will change to some degree. Therefore, the action she needs to take is going to change as well.

Balance of Power

We frequently hear the term "balance of power" in the context of international relations. Some event may be reported, for example, as threatening the balance of power in the Middle East. Balance of power, however, is also often an issue in interpersonal relations, even though it is not the way we usually think about our interactions with other individuals. Much like *imbalance* is a useful way to think about your problem state, working from a perspective of *power imbalance* can help clarify what is going on between you and your other in almost any dramatic circumstance you might devise.

You want your dramatic circumstance to compel you to take action. At the same time, it is important that the action you choose to take be the most effective one for actually getting what you want from your other. When you think that "winning" is going to require an adjustment of the power balance between you and your other, you will gravitate toward choices that will be more effective.

Using my story about getting money from my father to attend the summer workshop as an example, remember that even though what my father was saying was very hurtful and made me want to lash out, I had to keep in mind that the only communication that would likely have any impact had to be reasonable and "adult." That is because the natural power imbalance between parent and child needed to be adjusted by me behaving like a grown-up. Otherwise, from my father's perspective, my argument could easily be damaged if I were behaving in any way that he could think of as childish or immature. That kind of behavior would, in fact, most likely strengthen his resolve to remain "parental" and protect me from decisions I was making as the result of my immaturity and lack of knowledge.

If Joanne were singing to her mother, she would be well advised to consider behavior that would also take into account the power imbalance that always exists to some degree or another between a parent and a child, no matter how old the child may be. If Joanne is able to be perceived by her mother as a grown-up, her mother is more likely to take her seriously and more likely to offer the kind of support Joanne is seeking. The power imbalance with her father is likely even greater, as her father might be much less tolerant of what he perceives as "weakness." Joanne might need to stand her ground a bit more forcefully to make sure that she will be heard and respected by her father.

If Joanne is singing to the man who actually left her, the balance of power is shifted almost totally in his favor. A friend of mine who is very wise about human relations and very, very wise about acting once told me, "Whoever says 'no' wins." If in Joanne's story she is going to sing to the guy who rejected her in the first place, she faces the very real possibility that he might reject her again. Because she has never recovered from his departure, she is going to be in an extremely vulnerable position, and her instincts are going to tell her that regardless of how honest she is willing to be about her feelings, she must, at the same time, provide herself with some level of protection. Otherwise, she is going to make herself even more vulnerable to the guy who left her than she already was in the first place. That is not something anyone who is actually in that kind of situation is going to do willingly.

Why does this matter? It matters most because actors so often love the idea that they are going to open themselves up and reveal their hearts. In real life, however, people do that in only the rarest, and usually safest, of circumstances. Stripping yourself "naked" may actually be required in a circumstance where you are desperate to get what you want and have no alternative. Even so, baring one's soul is always going to be your character's alternative of last resort.

Only actors think that suffering is fun, and while you certainly get to have a great deal of fun in any circumstance that causes you to suffer and reveal your soul, it is important that you keep in mind that the character you are playing has no desire to do either of those things. If an audience perceives that you are too willingly revealing every part of yourself—going to these most painful places with no discernible effort to avoid them—they will know that you are not behaving truthfully. The illusion of truth that is essential to the story you are telling will be lost.

Our work is always dependent on our audiences' willing suspension of disbelief. They are usually willing to play along and live inside the story right along with us. We need to make certain that we are helping them do that by not behaving in ways that strike them, either consciously or unconsciously, as contradictory to normal human behavior.

Scared Is a Good Thing

A student once gave me a thank-you card with a quote from Eleanor Roosevelt on the front that read, "Do one thing every day that scares you." Mrs. Roosevelt's advice for living the fullest kind of life certainly applies to an actor who wants to explore the fullest possible circumstance. The student who gave me the card was keenly aware that the most valuable work she and I had done together was the work that got her to take on and explore so many different things that she was afraid of.

The possibilities for danger in Joanne's dramatic circumstance are almost endless. She could be in a new relationship with a man she cares about deeply but finds herself so damaged by what happened in her last relationship that she is not able to make a commitment. She could have a sister who backs her into a corner saying, "Something is really wrong with you, and I'm not leaving until you tell me what it is!" She could be on the verge of losing her job because she's missed so much work, and her boss gives her one last chance to explain what is going on. And her boss could be someone she really likes, or really hates.

The best choice for an I-am-at-the-end-of-my-rope song such as "Autumn" will always be whatever puts the singer in the greatest danger. You put yourself in danger, and then you must be brave enough to take an action that you hope will protect you from that danger and ultimately make things better. It will take all the courage Joanne has to try to get what she wants from the man who left her and broke her heart, but she will do it anyway.

Why will she put herself at such risk? Because taking that risk is the only possible chance she has of mending her broken heart. A breaking heart is something with which every person in the world can identify. What attracts people to this kind of story is not the pain that a character is going through but the way in which the character copes with the pain. They want to see someone fight it and triumph over it. That is what interests us as an audience, because that is what frightens us, and we want to learn about how to cope with those fears.

As you explore your dramatic circumstances and envision living in different kinds of stories, you must be willing to challenge yourself by making the most dangerous choices, and creating an other who is a real threat is as good a place to start as any. Choose an other who is saying no to you, or someone who might well say no. If you have something precious, choose an other who is trying to take it away from you. Be brave enough to choose someone who might break your heart, or break it all over again. That is worth doing, and it is certainly worth watching.

Performers are lucky. There is always a ready opportunity to do something scary. Danger, in fact, lurks behind every corner. Just keep on reminding yourself that this is a game you are choosing to play, and you are doing it because it is fun. Making choices that put you in dangerous situations is how you will grow as an actor, and more importantly, it is how you will learn to be brave. Bravery, I have learned over the years, is definitely an acquired skill.

12

Choosing Yourself as Your Other

In the previous chapter, as Joanne began to think about who her strongest choice for an other might be, her first thought was that she was singing to herself. It is, in fact, often the case that the characters you portray will be singing to themselves, and that is what we are going to take a look at in this chapter.

Characters in musicals and operas are often alone on stage. Those times are frequently the most dramatic and powerful moments of the piece. When you find yourself in such a circumstance, it is still best to begin your analysis, just as Joanne did, by exploring all of the possibilities for an external other. That approach will encourage you to explore a wider range of possibilities, and it will help you delve into the complexities of the situation in which you find yourself. If, having done that, singing to yourself seems like the most logical and powerful choice you can make, you still want to maintain the idea that you are singing to an external other. Remember that every solo needs to be a scene.

I find that the best way to identify an external other when you are singing to yourself is to look at the situation as one in which your psyche has split in two. You play a game in which you have a temporary case of multiple personality disorder, and you ask yourself the following question: "Which part of myself is in conflict with which other part of myself?"

The Mother of All Monologues

Hamlet is certainly alone when he begins what is arguably the best-known soliloquy in the history of the theatre with the words "To be or not to be. That is the question." Hamlet is, in fact, talking to himself.

To which part of himself is Hamlet talking? Hamlet is speaking to his weaker self, the part of him that is reluctant to act.

And which part is doing the talking? Hamlet's stronger self is trying to persuade his weaker self to take action in response to his father's death. Hamlet needs his weaker, more reluctant self to join forces with his stronger, more determined self in order to become a unified entity. Because he feels split in two, he needs to bring these two parts of himself, both of which have credible voices, into an entity that is capable of taking action, an entity that can "be." The important thing to realize here is that this is not, for Hamlet, an internal struggle. It is not something happening inside his head. If it were, there would be no need to speak the words out loud. This is an external interaction between two opposing forces.

Shakespeare's great soliloquy is an argument between a man's stronger self and a man's weaker self. You could also say, if you are rooting for the weaker self, that it is an argument between a man's brash self and his wiser self. Because wouldn't it be wiser to accept the status quo and not stir up any trouble? Any actor who assumes the role of Hamlet must understand the nature of this kind of conflict, or he will run the risk of burying Hamlet's struggle inside himself so as to make that struggle, which does happen to be the very essence of the play, inaccessible to the audience.

This split-personality state is not uncommon even in less dramatic circumstances. People often experience this kind of split between what the heart wants to do and what the head is telling them to do. We struggle with what our conscience tells us is the right thing to do as our desires are leading us in the opposite direction. Our experienced self is smart enough not to fall in love with an unacceptable object of our affection, while the heart and other organs of the body leap quite happily into that sea of trouble. We can all identify with circumstances in which characters must struggle with conflicting parts of themselves, and we surely recognize that no one is comfortable in those kinds of circumstances.

It is, to say the least, disconcerting to find oneself in such a state, and if we do not find a resolution to the conflict—if you do not find some way to restore balance—we can sink into a state of anxiety-ridden inertia. Therefore, the only way to escape this particular kind of discomfort, other than using alcohol or drugs or some panacea to make the unresolved conflict go away, is to actively try to resolve the conflict. The two conflicting parts of ourselves will either come to agreement or, as is more often the case, one part will ultimately triumph over the other. One part of your psyche will simply overpower the other part of your psyche in order for you to be able to make a choice and move forward. Whether or not the choice you make is a good choice depends on the circumstances of the story you are telling. In comedies and romances, the choices usually lead to a happy ending. In tragedies, such as *Hamlet*, things tend not to work out quite as well.

We not only recognize this conflict in ourselves, but we can also readily see when it is happening to others, and we are most eager to see the outcome of this particular kind of hard-fought battle. The outcome of such struggles determines what action will be taken, and that action is usually what will propel the character in a story into the next conflict. As Hamlet's insistent self wins the battle with his reluctant self, he embarks on a course of action that will lead inevitably to his destruction.

Struggles such as this are the essence of real drama. Remember: it is the struggle that will energize you and empower you, and it is the struggle with which your audience will identify. Your audience does not need you to win. They need you to try.

The Soliloquy of All Soliloquies

Let's look at a coaching in which Sean is exploring the idea of choosing himself as his other. The song is Billy Bigelow's "Soliloquy" from *Carousel*, the Rodgers and Hammerstein musical adaption of the Ferenc Molnar play *Liliom*. If "To be or not to be" is the best-known soliloquy in the history of the theatre, "Soliloquy" from *Carousel* is arguably the best-known "monologue" in the history of musical theatre. At the point in the story when the song occurs, Billy has just found out that his wife is going to have a baby, and he is left alone to sort out how he feels about the life-altering news he has just received. Sean sang the song, which is just under eight minutes long, and we began our coaching.

WW: So. How was that?

S: Long.

WW: It felt long to you.

S: Well, it's such a huge event.

WW: What's huge about it?

S: The dramatic journey. The vocal journey. It's a lot of work.

WW: How do you feel about it vocally?

S: Pretty good. I have to keep my head on straight, or I'll have trouble at the end.

WW: What does keeping your head on straight entail?

S: I have to keep thinking and breathing.

WW: And those are the same things Billy is trying to do in the midst of his struggle. He's trying to keep thinking and trying to keep breathing.

S: That's true.

WW: So if we keep Billy focused, it's going to help us keep Sean focused.

S: And vice versa.

WW: You got it. Tell me about your circumstance.

S: Billy has just found out that his wife, Julie, is going to have a baby. She leaves him alone, and he sings this song.

WW: *You* sing this song.

S: Right. *I* sing it.

WW: And why do you sing it? What's your problem?

S: I'm really scared.

WW: What are you scared of?

S: Everything it means to be a father. I don't have a job. I go out every night and get drunk. I'm not very nice to my wife.

WW: And those things don't seem to add up to good parenting skills?

S: Exactly.

WW: This is all good problem stuff. Potent language. To whom are you singing?

S: Myself.

WW: Why's that?

S: Well, the song is called "Soliloquy."

WW: That's a pretty good indicator. So what are you actually *doing* as you sing to yourself? What action are you taking?

S: Er... thinking, musing.

WW: And are those actions, thinking and musing, powerful enough to take you all the way through this long song and into the life-changing and ultimately tragic choices you are going to make at the end of it?

S: Um... I think the answer to that would be no.

Billy is left alone after learning that he is going to be a father, and the struggle that ensues is expressed in a song. However, Billy is not simply musing. He is not reflecting or dreaming or engaged in any other kind of meditative activity that would let the singer see Billy as consumed by an internal struggle where he can lose himself in a series of adjectives that only add up to "thoughtful." Billy's behavior is not introverted, and the singer must find a vocabulary and an articulation of Billy's circumstance that is going to spur him to action.

WW: So... what are we going to do?

S: I really do think that I'm singing to myself.

WW: I agree.

S: Doesn't that mean that I'm thinking about it?

WW: Yes. And are you thinking out loud?

S: Well, yes. Actually, very out loud.

WW: It's like you're arguing, right?

S: Right.

WW: So what part of yourself is arguing with what other part of yourself?

S: What do you mean?

WW: Think of yourself as split into two different people. Who would those two people be in this particular circumstance?

S: I guess the part of me that thinks I'll be a good father and the part that thinks I'll be a terrible father.

WW: Excellent. Let's talk a bit more about the part that wants to be a good father. Why did you marry Julie?

S: Because I loved her.

WW: Do you still love her?

S: Yes, but I'm not doing a very good job of showing it.

WW: Do you want to?

S: Yeah. I wish that I could be a good husband and a good provider. I wish I could really believe that I'm capable of doing that.

WW: What keeps you from believing that?

S: My experience. All the things I've done in my life that aren't good.

WW: So how would you identify these two parts of you that are in conflict?

S: The part of me that wants to believe something is arguing with the part of me that knows that I'm probably going to fail.

WW: That's perfect! The part of you that wishes you could believe is singing to the part of you that knows better. Your hopeful self is singing to your cynical self.

S: Like one of those cartoons where the guy has a little angel on one shoulder telling him to be good and a little devil on the other telling him to be bad.

WW: That's the idea. Except in this case, you are the little angel who is actually arguing with—fighting with—the little devil.

Billy is engaged in a battle between the good part of himself that wants to believe in home and happiness and the bad part that refuses to acknowledge that possibility. Those are the bad and good terms in which Billy sees himself, because that is the way the world has always seen him. He finds himself moved by the news that he is going to be a father, and somewhat to his surprise, he actually longs to embrace this news and fully acknowledge that this child will be a physical manifestation of his deep love for Julie. But the cynical Billy, the one whom life has all too often kicked in the teeth, stands outside the dumbstruck Billy, insisting that fatherhood for Billy Bigelow is a ludicrous prospect.

This all appears to be pretty straightforward. It is the good guy versus the bad guy. Life, however, is not that simple, and that is particularly true with the kind of intense internal conflict that rises to a level where it manifests itself externally in words or in a song. Characters such as Billy Bigelow and Hamlet do not find themselves in these situations by accident, and in stories of this nature, things are usually more complicated than good vs. evil. Both of these characters, bear in mind, end up dead.

WW: Do you dislike the devil part of you?

S: I love it!

WW: Do you mean as you or as Billy?

S: As Sean.

WW: So what about Billy. Does he like the devil in him?

S: It sounds like I should say no.

WW: But you don't want to?

S: No.

WW: Why not?

S: There are a lot of things about myself I really like.

WW: Let's talk about those things.

S: Well...I see myself as kind of a renegade. I don't want to play by other people's rules. I'm independent.

WW: And those aren't bad things.

S: No.

WW: How'd you get that way?

S: I figure that I had a really rough time as a kid and had to start fighting for myself at a really young age. That's really all I know.

WW: Where does the angel part of you come from?

S: Well...I do really love Julie, and when I'm with her it seems possible that I could lead a different kind of life. I think she could give me a home and a family and all of the things that I didn't have when I was growing up.

WW: And what does the devil have to say about that?

S: That I'm crazy. Things are never going to change for me.

WW: How long has this battle been going on?

S: Probably forever.

WW: Why does it suddenly erupt as it does in this song?

S: Because the stakes are higher. If I screw up, I always figure that at some level Julie can take care of herself, but a baby can't do that.

WW: So the conflict becomes what?

S: It becomes a crisis. I can't move forward until something gets figured out.

WW: Why is the song so long?

S: I wish I knew!

WW: It takes as long as it takes for Billy to make a decision.

S: It takes that long for one side to win?

WW: Or to declare itself the winner. What do you decide to do?

S: To steal the money I need to take care of the baby.

WW: So who wins?

S: Nobody.

WW: Why not?

S: Because I stop thinking. The pressure gets so great that I just declare what I'm going to do, and then I go about it all wrong. I make a really stupid decision.

WW: And that decision, one that is made for all sorts of good reasons, leads to what?

S: My death.

WW: And that's what is at the heart of a tragedy and what makes for a true tragic hero: bad decisions made for good reasons.

Sean then took the time he needed to prepare and center and envision the conflict that was going on between the two parts of himself. He sang the song again, and after he was finished, I asked for feedback from students in the class.

St#1: That didn't seem long at all.

WW: I agree. Why not?

St#1: He was dealing with each thing just as it came along, and it made me always want to know what was going to happen next.

Singers often complain that a song is too long or that the lyrics are repetitive. In some cases that is true, but more often than not a song seems long because the singer has not figured out the actual journey that needs to be taken. If you look at "Soliloquy" and determine that it starts with a pensive part and then gets joyful and defiant and then gets worried and sentimental and then gets upset and angry, you are going to have a very long song on your hands, and so will the people listening to you.

St#2: I've heard this song sung lots of times, but there were certain words that I had never heard before today.

WW: That happened to me as well. In fact, that is always an indicator to me that the singer is really living inside the circumstance of the song.

St#1: The words came alive in a different way.

WW: Why's that?

St#1: Because Sean was using them so specifically to get the thing he wanted.

WW: And that's what this work is all about.

The Showstopper

Given both the vocal and dramatic demands of "Soliloquy," combined with the fact that it occupies a position as a kind of "Mount Everest" for high baritones, this is probably as good a time as any to talk about the really big songs. I do not think there is a singer alive who has not run a movie of himself or herself standing center stage bringing down the house as the theatre reverberates with the glorious sound of a series of high notes that represent the epitome of vocal and dramatic excellence. These are the anthems and arias that when successfully performed are the singer's equivalent of hitting a home run with the bases loaded. These are the "showstoppers."

I am sure you know the kind of song I am talking about. The list would include "Anthem" from *Chess*, "Gethsemane" from *Jesus Christ Superstar*, "The Story Goes On" from *Baby*, "Meadowlark" from *The Baker's Wife*, "Defying Gravity" from *Wicked*, "Bring Him Home" from *Les Misérables*, "I Dreamed a Dream" from *Les Misérables*, and assorted other songs from *Les Misérables*. These songs, and many others like them, are thrilling to audiences and performers alike, and singers often approach them determined to "thrill." And that is a recipe for disaster.

What is your first job when approaching a "big" song? Your first job is to make it little.

Just what does that mean? It means that, in life, anyone with a really big problem is, in fact, trying very hard to make that problem smaller. When confronted with challenging circumstances, we try to face them by sorting out the challenge into more manageable parts. When confronted with a truly heightened or dangerous circumstance, we tell ourselves to calm down. We make ourselves breathe. We try to think in order to come up with a way out of the problem we are in. And that is exactly what the singer of any big song needs to do.

Billy tries in a very logical way to sort through what is for him a perilous situation, and in the process he comes to a decision that is even more perilous. In other words, he fails. That is what makes the song so powerful. The decisions that Billy makes in the course of the song are ultimately driven by his fear and by his pride, which is not the kind of thinking that is very helpful when one is dealing with such life-altering circumstances. The "bigness" of the song is the result of Billy's failure to make the problem small. No matter how hard he tries, he cannot keep the problem under his control. Like any person dealing with any emotional situation that is fraught with peril, Billy's goal is to not give in to his fear, but that, in the end, is exactly what he does. It is Billy's struggle to win while he is actually losing that is going to make the song reach a certain size. And this is something, given the nature of the story and the text and the music, that will happen to any actor playing Billy who is actually able to live inside the story. It is not something he has to make happen.

Heart vs. Head

Whenever you find yourself working with a dramatic circumstance that indicates you are singing to yourself, the conflict is almost always some manifestation of your heart doing battle with your head. The struggles between head and heart, mind and body, practicality and romanticism are at the core of the best stories.

Billy's hopeful self, with its romantic view of how life might be with his new child, struggles with his cynical self, the logical part of his nature whose experience tells him that this situation is not going to turn out well. The song gets bigger because Billy must finally drown out the voices of doubt and declare that he will make this situation come out okay, or he will die trying.

Hamlet's courageous self, driven by his love for his father and his inability to accept the injustice of his father's death, is in conflict with his frightened self, the part of him driven by the practical knowledge that he has little power and is likely to fail at any attempt to change his current circumstances. Hamlet's brain tells him not to head down this dangerous path, but his heart will not be dissuaded.

It is human nature, as we observe struggles such as these, to want the heart to win. We hope that against all odds these characters will triumph in their struggle for the things they want and the things they want to believe in. When they fail, we experience that failure as if it were our own. That makes good theatre. We also want the heart to win because so often in our own lives it is not our hearts that make the final decision. We choose what is wiser and safer, and it is probably a good thing that we do. That, however, makes us long all the more for stories in which the characters risk everything for love, whatever form that love may take. The outcome in stories such as these may be predictable, but we still find the struggle exciting. You can find this kind of struggle compelling in the dramatic circumstances you occupy, and your audiences will find it compelling as they watch you engage in that struggle.

There are many reasons why you should value the idea of *struggle*, but the main reason is that struggle is something you can actually *do*. It is something you can act.

13

Pursuing
Your Objective

In acting school I was taught that it was very important to concentrate, and though I was a model student and especially good at following directions, my problem with this particular instruction was that I could not figure out what to concentrate on. I am more than somewhat embarrassed to admit it, but I spent a great deal of time on stage repeating the word *concentrate* over and over in my head. That was, as I am sure you can imagine, not what my teachers had in mind, nor was it the least bit helpful. It was, in fact, every bit as useless as repeating the word *relax* over and over in my head, since relaxing was also something I was supposed to be doing. However you look at it, it was obvious to me that little progress was being made if while repeating these words in a nonstop cycle I was dropping lines and missing entrances. As bizarre as it seems in retrospect, I really could not figure it out. I know now that the problem was that I was so busy watching myself that there was no room left for me to watch the other people on stage, the other characters in the story that should have been the object of my focus.

What *do* you concentrate on? You concentrate on your objective.

How do you figure out what your objective is? You play "what if." You take the time to step inside your story, and from that perspective you allow yourself to imagine what it would be like to face the same challenges that your character is facing. Your heart and your gut will then reveal to you just what it is you must do to address those challenges.

There were any number of dedicated teachers throughout my years of training who gave me lots and lots of things to concentrate on. Their instructions were for the most part valid and always well intended. However, in my self-conscious and unfocused state, the things I was supposed to be concentrating on would morph into a list of "shoulds," and while I was busy checking my "should" list and checking it twice, I really was not accomplishing very much in the way of actual acting.

One teacher's voice, I have to say, managed to penetrate my confusion and stay with me over the years. Leonard would ask, "What do you want?" In fact, he asked it so often that I sometimes wondered if asking that question was all Leonard actually knew how to do. I would lose my sense of where I was in a scene, and Leonard would ask me, "What do you want?" A monologue would feel awkward and lacking in any forward momentum, and he would repeat his question, "What do you want?" A really good performance would be followed the next day by a not-so-good performance of the same material, and Leonard would be there at the ready with another "What do you want?"

What happened as a result of Leonard's insistence that I answer the question? The good news is that it often led to very interesting conversations, from which I was able to gain some insight into what it was that I wanted. The bad news is that I was not all that good at actually pursuing the thing I wanted, even after I had figured out just what that thing was. I was too caught up in getting things "right" and trying to be "good" to fully commit myself to an action. Many actors find it challenging, if not impossible, to articulate what it is exactly that they want. This can be true in life as well as in acting. Many actors also find it difficult to commit to an action. The dramatic circumstance process is the best way I have found for surmounting both of those challenges.

There is an old story that people like to tell about Bette Davis. She was in rehearsal with a younger, less experienced actor, and the actor stopped in the middle of a line and turned to the director to ask, "What is my motivation?" Bette jumped right in with, "Your paycheck!" There are two things as far as I am concerned that are wrong with this story. First, it dismisses—actually makes fun of—the legitimate steps that actors must take in asking themselves what they are doing and why they are doing it. The second thing that is wrong with the story, and why I imagine that it never actually happened, is that Bette Davis demonstrated in film after film her ability to pursue an objective with a sense of all-consuming need and single-mindedness that made her one of the most powerful actors in the history of film.

Whenever we pursue an objective, both when we are acting and in real life, we naturally become less self-conscious. Focusing our attention on a goal we want to achieve makes us more present in our circumstances. We respond to what is happening more immediately and spontaneously. Without having to think about it, we engage more of our instrument, and we participate more fully in the activity at hand. We worry less about how we are doing because we are so focused on doing it, and sometimes we do not worry at all. Worrying and being distracted when trying to perform are perhaps the biggest challenges that an actor faces. They are the things that most often derail what might otherwise be very good work. Remember Charlotte and her "committee"?

In addition to watching ourselves and distracting ourselves, we also have a tendency to try to pursue several different things at the same time. If you are playing baseball and the coach tells you to keep your eye on the ball, there is no doubt as to what that ball is. You know what a baseball looks like, and you understand what it means to keep your eye on it. The acting "baseball" can be much more elusive. Because the training you go through and the skills you employ when you perform are made up of so many different parts, it can feel as if you are being asked to keep your eye on more than one ball at a time, and before long there can be way too many balls flying fast and furious and threatening to hit you in the head.

So what are you supposed to do? You make one thing the focus of your attention and your energy. You pursue that one thing with such a level of commitment that other things start to take care of themselves.

There is no doubt that when people focus intently on what they want to achieve, they are frequently able to surprise themselves, and the people watching them, with just how far their determination and strength of purpose can take them. There are many stories of people performing extraordinary feats simply because they were compelled to do so, such as a mother who was able to pull the door off of a burning car in order to save her baby who was trapped inside. The mother's need to rescue her child fueled her determination to do the one thing that she knew would save her child's life, and it gave her superhuman strength that under normal circumstances she would never have had. Rescuing a baby from a burning car may be an extreme example of the power of motivation, but it is actually a useful model for the most effective way to think about your dramatic circumstances. In any moment when your character knows exactly what is wanted or needed, there should be nothing else in the world that is more important. The thing you want is your objective, and why you want it is your motivation. Together they make up the most effective tool you have in your actor toolkit.

A book that I highly recommend is *A Practical Handbook for the Actor* by Melissa Bruder et al. (Vintage, 1986). The authors employ a vocabulary that I think is very helpful in reminding actors that they must always stay focused on their objective. They say that every action must have a *test*.

> The test of the action must be in the other person. An action is the physical pursuance of a specific goal, and that specific goal must have to do with the other person. In other words, by looking at your partner, you should be able to tell how close you are to completing your action.

A test of an action is the specific thing that tells you whether your action has succeeded or failed. It is a way of looking at your objective that will keep you focused on the success of your actions rather than the success of your work. The most effective way to make your objective specific is to ask yourself, "What do I want my other to do?"

In a recent coaching of Stephen Sondheim's "On the Steps of the Palace" from *Into the Woods*, a singer changed her objective from getting her judgmental other to understand why she made the choices she had made to wanting to get her judgmental other to agree with and approve the choices. Her other's approval, whatever form that might take, became the *test* for the action. The singer then reported back to me after she had gone back and listened to the recording of her coaching: "It's strange, because when I listen to the song the first time I sang it through, it seems pretty connected, but then when you had me start again, it was just so much more. You helped me refine my objective just a little bit more, and from the very beginning, it changed from me simply making statements to me engaging in my argument. Every single phrase seemed to have a purpose and intention. Instead of describing the prince, I am using his cleverness as part of my explanation and my defense."

Defining Your Objective

Shane is working on the song "And They're Off" from William Finn's musical *A New Brain*, in which the story's main character talks about what it was like growing up with an irresponsible father who constantly fought with his mother, gambled away all the family's money, and ultimately abandoned his wife and child.

My goal in this coaching was to intensify Shane's dramatic circumstance in order to get the "size" of the circumstance to be equal to the "size" of the song. While you should never think that it is your job to get bigger, you can absolutely work to make your problem bigger and your objective more compelling so that your need to take action will be more specific, immediate, and compelling.

WW: Shane, what is your circumstance?

S: Well, in the show I'm suffering from a brain disorder and facing surgery that will either save my life or kill me.

WW: And why do you sing this song?

S: I think I'm just thinking about my life and reflecting on what it was like growing up with a really bad father.

WW: And to whom are you singing?

S: Well, I decided to take it out of the context of the show and sing it to my girlfriend.

WW: And why sing it to her?

S: Because I want her to understand what I went through as a kid.

WW: And why does she need to understand that?

S: I want to be closer to her.

WW: You want to be closer to her, so you are going to tell her all about your father.

S: Right.

WW: And does the song itself seem to support that objective?

S: Not exactly.

WW: What's different?

S: I get pretty upset.

WW: Why's that?

S: Because my relationship with my father was terrible, and it's hard to talk about these things.

WW: So, if you decided that you wanted to tell your girlfriend about your unhappy upbringing because you wanted her to know you better, you would probably not use this language or tell these kinds of stories.

S: Not if they were going to upset me.

WW: Right. So can you imagine a circumstance in which you would have no choice but to tell your girlfriend about this?

S: The relationship could be getting pretty serious, and she wants to meet my parents.

WW: And you don't want her to?

S: Not my dad.

WW: Okay. You've already got a more potent circumstance. You're imagining that your girlfriend wants to meet your parents.

S: My actual girlfriend?

WW: We're making up a story. You put your girlfriend in it, I assume, because you wanted to be singing to someone who means something to you.

S: Right.

WW: So we're using that as a jumping-off point for an imaginary circumstance. We're going to play the "what if" game. You already began it when you suggested, "She wants to meet my parents."

S: She's already met my parents.

WW: Right, so now we're imagining. We've started with someone you care about, your girlfriend, and we're creating a more dramatic circumstance. It's not real. It's a game.

S: Why does she want to meet my parents?

WW: You tell me.

S: Well, it's usually a sign that the relationship is getting serious.

WW: Good. She thinks that you introducing her to your parents will mean that you take the relationship seriously.

S: Got it.

WW: Why don't you want her to meet your dad?

S: Because he's a jerk, and I don't want anything to do with him.

WW: So right now I'm going to talk to you as if I were your girlfriend.

S: Okay.

WW: "You mean that I'm never supposed to meet your father?"

S: That's what I mean.

WW: "You hate him that much?"

S: I...I just don't want to see him.

WW: "That can't be good for you."

S: He did terrible things to me and my mother.

WW: "And you're never going to forgive him?"

S: I don't want to.

WW: "But you're the one who is going to pay the price for that! You can't carry this around with you your whole life."

S: I bet I can.

WW: "Not if I have anything to say about it."

S: Yikes.

WW: So, Shane. What do you need to do now?

S: I need to make her understand what it was like growing up around my father so that she will be willing to stay in the relationship.

WW: And will that force you to talk about things you don't want to talk about?

S: Yep.

WW: We've imagined a circumstance that now makes you have to do what the character actually does in this song. You have to revisit these painful experiences in order to try to somehow free yourself of them.

S: But I don't think he does free himself.

WW: It doesn't matter. It's the effort that engages us. It's the struggle that creates conflict and drama and makes you take action.

S: I'm doing it for my girlfriend.

WW: Right. You don't want to somehow sacrifice your relationship with her to your terrible childhood. Your "what if" brings you into the circumstance in a more immediate way. Can you take that further? What if you and your girlfriend were getting married and you were refusing to invite your father to the wedding.

S: That's intense on several levels.

WW: That's the goal. What are some of those levels?

S: She thinks that I must be a really cold person if I can just cut my dad out of my life, and she's afraid that I could someday treat her that way.

WW: Or your children.

S: Aaagh! This just gets worse and worse.

WW: In the song you talk about your parents fighting to the point where they draw blood, right?

S: Right.

WW: That tells me that there has got to be something pretty powerful going on in your story to make you revisit that. What is it that's actually happening in the story of the show?

S: I think I'm going to die.

WW: What is happening in the story you are devising?

S: I'm going to lose the woman that I love.

WW: And the moment you realize you are going to lose her, your subconscious mind makes no distinction between that and dying.

S: So this is how I could think about my circumstance if I were in the show and had to imagine that kind of loss.

WW: Right. And what do you want your fiancée to do?

S: Let me off the hook about my dad.

WW: And how will you know when she's done that?

S: I have to look at her, and see what she's doing.

WW: As compared to...?

S: As compared to what I want her to be doing.

WW: What would that look like—literally look like?

S: She would...see me differently. She would suddenly understand what I went through as a kid and would not push me about my father.

WW: And how will you know when that has happened—*if* that has happened?

S: She could say it.

WW: You're right. She could say, "Shane, now that I understand what your childhood was like I will no longer push you about your father." How likely is that?

S: Not very.

WW: Why not?

S: Because people don't really say things like that.

WW: So take the time to figure out what she might do. This is the point in creating your circumstance—that you take the time to explore your "what if" in as fully realized a manner as possible. You release your jaw. You center, and you breathe. You envision yourself in your circumstance, and you allow your problem to live in your breath and to move into the center of your body. You envision your other, and you watch her respond to the things that you are telling her. Create the scene in your head. Make the movie of this girl suddenly realizing that she is in love with you. Maintain your focus and keep breathing. Tell me what she is doing.

S: She's starting to turn away but then she stops. She looks at me—looks kind of surprised, like she just saw something she had never seen before. She seems to want to ask me a question but doesn't say anything. Then she starts walking toward me, slowly and deliberately, and when she gets right next to me she puts her arms around my neck and kisses me.

WW: How does she kiss you?

S: Like she means it!

WW: Perfect. Now you have an objective and now you are ready to sing the song.

Shane now has an objective. He knows everything that he wants the girl that he loves to do, and he knows that he will have succeeded only when he gets kissed "like she means it!" By focusing all of his attention on her and how she responds—or does not respond—Shane can ascertain at any point along the way just how he is doing. The kiss is the "test" of his action. He will know how close he is to accomplishing his objective by whether or not he gets that kiss, and his actions will spontaneously adjust in order to evoke the response he wants from the girl. And remember, even though it is not Shane's job to express what he feels, his feelings will probably reveal themselves as he pursues his objective.

S: But what if it doesn't happen? What if she doesn't kiss me?

WW: Then your dramatic circumstance is even more powerful.

S: It's better if I lose?

WW: It's better if you have to keep working to achieve what you want to achieve.

S: What do you mean?

WW: What's the test of your action?

S: The kiss.

WW: Right. And once you've gotten that kiss, your dramatic circumstance is complete. Within the story you've created, once you've been kissed, there is no reason to keep singing. You will have accomplished your objective and, in doing so, will have eliminated any need to take action. You have to have an objective that takes you all the way to the end of your story.

S: It's the "trying" that makes the song compelling.

WW: Infinitely more compelling. And any circumstance in which you want to get kissed will be much more powerful if she never kissed you. That's the size of the game you need to be playing. Big songs require big problems, and the way to live inside that problem is to imagine a scenario that becomes increasingly problematic. You connect your story to your breath. You let the movie of that story run in your head, and you get your imaginative brain to play the game that you want to play.

Dramatic Structure

Your objective—what you want your other to do—grows out of your dramatic circumstance, and learning how to articulate and occupy a dramatic circumstance is the key to how you live inside your stories, bringing both the story and yourself to life. If you are in pursuit of an objective and are confronted with an obstacle, it is your desire to "win" that will propel you forward. Characters in the most powerful stories move forward at all costs, against all obstacles. That is what you want to be able to do in the roles you play. You want to move forward at all costs and against all obstacles.

What happens if you are in a public place and two people suddenly raise their voices and begin to argue? You watch them. You watch them because they are involved in something that is pushing them past the boundaries of normal behavior. Their need to get what they want has caused them to lose awareness of their surroundings, and because they are totally absorbed in their conflict, you become absorbed as well. We are fascinated by people who feel things strongly and who are willing to take action based on those feelings, and we always want to know who is going to win. That is drama. That is what people want to watch. It is human nature to be interested in people who are engaged in conflict, and conflict that rises to the level of drama will compel an audience to follow any story to its conclusion.

The source of all of drama is conflict. Conflict is, in fact, the only thing that makes a dramatic situation dramatic. Conflict occurs when different people want different things, and when these people interact as characters in a story, we have drama.

A textbook definition of drama is "a series of exciting, emotional, or unexpected events." So it follows that a dramatic circumstance is an exciting, emotional, or unexpected set of circumstances.

Drama is actually a Greek word that derives from the verb *dran*, which means "to do or to act," and the dramatic circumstance process is about discovering just what you need to do and what action you need to take.

The dramatic circumstance process is designed to lead you to the point where you are compelled to take action in order to achieve your objective. The process begins the moment you have a problem. In order to solve that problem, you decide there is something that you want—better yet, something that you must have. As you set out to get the thing you need, you become the *protagonist* in your dramatic circumstance. You will then encounter an obstacle to the thing you want, most often in the form of another person, and that person who stands in your way is your *antagonist*. You and your antagonist engage in a series of actions in which the conflict rises, and we have drama.

In a well-constructed drama, the conflict between protagonist and antagonist rises to the level of crisis. *Crisis* is the breaking point at which either the protagonist or the antagonist is going to prevail because neither can move forward until the conflict is resolved. Crisis then leads to *climax* and *resolution*. These dramatic elements—protagonist, antagonist, conflict, crisis, climax, and resolution—make up the fundamental template for dramatic structure, and good dramatic structure is the stuff that makes good stories, plays, movies, musicals, and operas. This paradigm of dramatic structure is traditionally used to analyze the structure of an entire play. A well-written scene, however, is built on the same dramatic principles, and sound dramatic structure is likewise inherent in any well-written monologue—or, for our purposes, any well-written song.

An understanding of the basic principles of dramatic structure will provide you with a methodology for analyzing any piece of dramatic material. It will help you figure out any story in which it is your job to assume the role of one of the characters. Just keep in mind that from your perspective as the actor, every character you play is the protagonist of your own story. You have to want something, and there has to be something preventing you from getting it. It is your identification of the dramatic components of the songs you sing that will allow you to utilize the power inherent in any dramatically well-structured story.

Your ability to articulate and occupy a dramatic circumstance will help you find clarity, immediacy, and action in all of your work. You want the clarity of knowing exactly what is happening in your story, and you want to utilize that clarity to be able to feel at your core, in your very center, what it would be like to be in a specific circumstance. The physical activation that comes out of the centering process brings the story to life in your body in an immediate way. That immediacy will evoke an impulse to take action.

Trust Your Instincts

You may have noticed that in presenting the elements of dramatic structure, I did not elaborate on conflict, crisis, climax, and resolution. There is a reason for that. I believe that the elements of conflict, crisis, climax, and resolution live within the material itself. They are there for you to experience, not to figure out or plan. This work is designed to create in you an irresistible impulse to take an action, and when your action is met with a response from your other, that response will create another impulse. That impulse does not come out of what you know you have to do. It comes out of what you know you have to get. Your job is to focus on the wanting so that the *wanting* will inspire the *doing*.

It is your occupation of your circumstance that will inspire you to take action. It will give you no choice but to take action. By exploring and committing to your problem, your other, and your objective, you will be compelled to take action, and taking action is what your work needs to be about. Once you have taken your initial action, it is the response you get—or do not get—that inspires the next action. That is what it means to live inside your story. You will discover the journey you need to take rather than plan it. Another way of saying it: let the writers do their job, and you do yours.

Identifying and pursuing what you want can be both liberating and empowering. It is what allows you to fully occupy a circumstance and, in doing so, connect to the dramatic power inherent in that circumstance. And if you are able to commit to your story to the point where you are unable to stop yourself from pursuing the thing you must have, you will have "hooked into" the power that is intrinsic to dramatic structure.

When you tap into this power, this energy, you *ride* it, much like a surfer rides a wave in the ocean. You are not in control of the journey, but you are in charge of it. The momentum of the water and the force of gravity are more powerful than any human being, and these unrelenting forces may knock you over at any time. However, with skill and experience, the accomplished surfer knows how to navigate to victory, much like you will navigate your way to achieving your objective. And you can take comfort in the fact that if you fail, at least your failure will be spectacular. It will be something worth watching.

Trust yourself enough to put something out in the world. Then allow yourself to respond to whatever comes back. The most important thing you can learn about yourself is that your instinctive responses will be sufficient. Those responses will, in fact, be you at your most powerful. They are you functioning as your most true and realized self. You have the stuff you need to do your work. You are enough.

When Singing Is Not Singing

Just as it was not Shane's job to express how he feels when singing "And They're Off," it was also not Shane's job, as the person inside the story, for him to sing it. That statement may sound strange, but from a storytelling perspective, singing just happened to be what Shane was going to do because that is the dramatic material he had in hand. Music was the medium through which he happened to be communicating. That is the case in almost any circumstance in any musical or opera. The character is not singing, even though you may be. The actor is singing because that is the medium. It is the "language" in which the piece has been written. Ideally the singing will appear inadvertent, as only a method for communication and not an end in itself.

I want you to learn how to find the one job you have to do and focus solely on that. We get caught up in too many things at one time. We try to serve too many masters, and we end up not really able to do our work. I want you to allow your voice, body, mind, and spirit to respond to your need to accomplish a task. When you are able to do that, you—and your work—will truly come to life. All of the parts of you and your craft will fall into place in service of getting the thing that you must have. That is a promise.

I have often wished I could revisit those years in acting school and take advantage of what Leonard and the other teachers there were asking me to do. While that is not possible, I am happy to report that throughout my post-acting-school years of performing, directing, writing, and teaching, Leonard's "What do you want?" stayed in my head. It had earned its place in my consciousness, and over time I was more and more able to answer that very important question and let the answer inform the actions I was going to take.

"What do you want?" is a specific step along the "what if" journey. You place yourself in a dramatic circumstance, and from within the circumstance, you identify what is wrong. Once you know what is wrong, you can figure out what might make it right. The thing that might "right your wrong" is the answer to your question, "What do I want?" This way of thinking works for me. I know it can work for you.

14

Playing the Brain Game

A year or so ago, a friend recommended I read *A General Theory of Love*, a book about how neural connections define our relationships and emotional connections with others, and how neural pathways are created in the brain that support those connections. I found the book, to say the least, interesting, and it occurred to me that many of the things the authors were writing about were relevant to the kind of work I was doing in my acting classes. Specifically, the triune brain theory, and its explanation of the various ways in which the various parts of our brain interact to influence our emotional lives, offered some potentially valuable insights into just why the dramatic circumstance process seemed to have so great an impact on so many students.

How interested should you be in brain science? That is entirely up to you. I find the connection both fascinating and useful. Thomas Lewis, Fari Amini, and Richard Lannon, the authors of *A General Theory of Love* (Vintage, 2001), express it this way:

Seekers of the heart's secrets might be tempted to detour around the essential facts of brain structure, fearing the subject is impossibly technical and probably soporific. It is not. No one disputes that the brain's dense, delicate, filamentous intricacy inspires awe, and more than occasionally dismay. Those who wish to drink in the details, however, need not drown in them. Anybody can operate a car without an engineering degree.

The dramatic circumstance process asks that you organize your thoughts in a particular way and then connect those thoughts to your breath and body. Once your breath and body are brought into play, they exert their own influence over the process. This back-and-forth connection allows you to "live" inside the story you are telling and experience a sense of immediacy in both your objectives and your interaction with the other character(s) in your story. In other words, this process shows you how to choose the most productive ways of thinking in order to stimulate your most productive work. It is about how you prepare, and it is intended to answer some of the most important questions singers and actors ask themselves every day. How do I best prepare to sing? How do I best prepare to act? How do I best prepare to do both at the same time?

I have worked with singers and actors every day for over forty years. I say "every day" because I count the time I spend thinking, and I count that time because I have learned over the past forty years that the way we *think* about things determines how we *do* those things. I know this to be true of my work, and I know it to be true of yours.

When you get up to sing and act, you, of course, want to do well. The good news is that what you do, and how well you do what you do, will always be a product of how you have organized your thoughts in the course of your preparation. However, as is so often the case, the good news is also the bad news. Each and every time you perform, the thoughts in your head are going to determine what is going to come out of your mouth. That sounds simple enough. Think good thoughts and get good results. But what are "good" thoughts? How do you put them in your head? How do you keep them there? What about all of the other thoughts, all the not-so-good thoughts that can enter unbidden and start making so much noise?

The human brain is an amazing thing. It is capable of guiding us through complex pathways to profound realizations and astounding achievement. It is also capable of looping the same eight bars of music inside our heads for hours on end and telling us at any given moment that the best course of action would be to chuck everything and go out for ice cream. It would be nice if we could control our thoughts. We are, in fact, often told that the control of our mind is the pathway to our success. But the human brain resists being controlled. Your brain does not, if you will pardon the expression, think that way.

At the same time, however, the human brain is very open to suggestion. It can be guided and focused. It can be seduced. The human brain likes to play. It likes to imagine things. It loves a good story and will readily transport itself—and transport you—to beautiful places, dangerous places, and exciting places. If you can imagine something, your brain can bring it to life.

And how do you get your brain to do that? You get it to do it by telling it to do it. You get your brain to play by giving it specific instructions. You organize your thoughts into a sequence of logical steps, and you train yourself and your mind to follow those steps whenever you do your work. You are not in control of your mind or your thoughts, and you are never going to be in control of your work. You can, however, be *in charge,* and those periods of time when you are in charge will be when you do your best singing and your best acting. At the risk of repeating myself, what you do and how well you do it will be the product of what you think.

Let me again quote playwright and author David Mamet's book *True and False* (Vintage, 1999).

> Our minds work with unbelievable speed assembling and ordering information. That is our protective device as animals, and it has enabled us both to defeat the wooly mammoth and to vote for supply-side economics—we are infinitely suggestible.

I believe that it is a boon to any actor to be able to take advantage of the brain's suggestibility, and the process of accessing those parts of the brain begins with breath and language. The key to everything is language: the actual words you use to articulate what is happening to you and what you are going to do. A language that is precise, powerful, and proactive makes all the difference in the world, because language is the way you have—the only way you have—of taking charge of your thoughts and truly engaging your brain. And by that I mean every part of your brain. It is through language that you persuade your cognitive brain to engage your imaginative brain and get it to play the game that you want to play. A playful brain is the actor's best friend, and it can be your best friend.

Many years ago I was told, "The subconscious mind has no sense of humor." This struck me then as meaningful information and a very useful idea for those of us who work in the theatre. Over the years it has proven itself true time and time again, and it has been invaluable in the development of the dramatic circumstance process. The ideas we plant in our subconscious mind are, as far as that particular part of our brain system is concerned, true.

In the March 1, 2010, edition of *The New Yorker*, Louis Menand, a professor of English at Harvard, published an article entitled "Head Case: Can Psychiatry Be a Science?" about the science of diagnosing and treating depression. Dr. Menand reports, "The brains of people who are suffering from mild depression look the same on a scan as the brains of people whose football team has just lost the Super Bowl. They even look the same as *the brains of people who have been asked to think sad thoughts* [italics mine]."

It would have been nice, from my acting-teacher perspective, if Dr. Menand had not used the word *sad* in that last sentence, because as an actor, you do know by now that it is dangerous to take on any emotional obligation as part of your work process. Setting that aside for the moment, Dr. Menand's report of this scientific data indicates that you can tell yourself a story and induce the same actual brain activity whether that story is real or imagined. And that is how—and why—I believe the "what if" game and the dramatic circumstance process actually work. Your subconscious mind evokes truthful responses and inspires action in circumstances that are entirely imaginary because at some level it does not realize that the circumstances are imaginary.

I find this to be a really exciting way to look at acting. While I do not think it is necessary that actors understand the actual brain function that makes it possible for them to live so truthfully inside their stories, I think it can be both interesting and valuable to explore that idea.

Shortly after I read *A General Theory of Love*, I had the good fortune to be invited to observe Marcia Lesser, a somatic experiencing practitioner and movement therapist, work with some of my program's students in an acting workshop. Marcia's field of study and practice focuses on how emotional connections are informed by the body. I observed Marcia guide the students to a mind/body consciousness that helped them tune into their nervous systems and stimulate their imaginations. I knew immediately that the work she was doing, and the way she talked about that work, could have a significant impact on the dramatic circumstance approach to acting.

Since that first meeting a little over two years ago, Marcia and I have worked with our faculty colleagues and students to explore how the knowledge and language of our two fields of study can be brought together to the benefit of our students. As Marcia explains it, "The mind/body connections are shared streams of energy and information that are endlessly flowing through the nervous system. These streams of energy and information influence, modify, and continuously affect each other."

Triune Brain Theory

Dr. Paul MacLean (1913–2007) was a neuroscientist and psychiatrist and the director of the Laboratory of Brain Evolution and Behavior at the United States National Institute of Mental Health. Dr. MacLean is best known for his "triune brain theory," in which he proposed that the three layers of the human brain developed through the process of evolution as the human organism became more complex and developed greater needs. He defined these three distinct layers as the reptilian brain, the limbic system, and the neocortex.

Just what are these three layers and what do they do? Marcia Lesser, being much more adept at the triune brain language than I, generously provided the following:

What follows is an updated version of the triune brain theory. Although Dr. MacLean believed the reptilian and limbic brains unconsciously influenced the cortex, the discovery of the flow—the give and take and plasticity between the regions—came years later. Each of the three regions has its own "conception" of the environment and each region responds accordingly. Depending on internal and external circumstances, a specific area may temporarily override the others, yet they are dependent on each other and ideally form one cohesive, whole brain.

The reptilian region is set deep within the structure of the brain. Also referred to as the brain stem, it was formed hundreds of millions of years ago. It is the home of instincts, and its "language" is sensation. It is encoded with the instinctual behaviors that maintain the survival of the species; it is from here that every higher life form has evolved. Your reptilian brain is fully wired and fully functioning at birth. When I think of this part of the brain, I picture a big lizard sunning itself on a rock. Hardwired to search for food and shelter, and to mate, it constantly scans for danger. There is no thought, just instinct.

Because it is so near to the spinal cord, the reptilian brain receives signals from the body and relays them to the limbic region and cortex. It also sends information back to the body. It controls our energy levels by regulating the heart, lungs, and digestive system, as well as our states of arousal, determining if we are hungry, tired, in danger, or sexually stimulated, as well as getting us ready for action. Aided by the evaluative ability of the limbic region and cortex, the reptilian brain coordinates how we respond to danger by mobilizing energy for the survival process of fight-flight-freeze. The primitive survival instinct to fight, flee, or freeze is involuntary. The strategy in the animal and human world is the same: the nervous system, alerted by the reptilian and limbic brains, prepares us to fight in the face of aggression or flee if winning the fight is not likely. The final defense, whenever these tactics don't ensure safety, is to freeze (immobility). In the animal world, the prey will literally play dead; predators are generally not interested in dead meat. Humans immobilize by dissociating: leaving their body and observing, not feeling, the danger and pain.

The limbic brain evolved two hundred million years ago when small mammals first appeared. All mammals have a reptilian core and a more elaborate limbic brain. It is the primary area of emotional and social behavior. The instinctual impulses of the reptilian brain are augmented here, the data complemented. It is here that our physical sensations are imbued with meaning: many neuroscientists believe that feelings are sensations originating in the body; emotions are evaluations of those feelings. Within the limbic region is the amygdala—the area that lets us know what to pay attention to, whether our experiences, external as well as internal, are safe. It plays a vital role in the activation of fear, "sounding the alarm" when a stimulus is perceived to be threatening. In this function, it works closely with the reptilian brain.

During the first eighteen months of a child's life, implicit memory (affective experiences, perceptions, sensations) is encoded without consciousness; the amygdala is a crucial part of this process. As we grow, the hippocampus, also in the limbic brain, comes into play, organizing sensory impressions into events: explicit memory. Memories at this stage are also autobiographical; we are able to think and talk about experiences that happened in the past.

The limbic region also includes the anterior cingulate, important because it registers physical sensations streaming from the reptilian brain. It also registers information from our social exchanges as well as regulating our focus and attention. It thus links body (reptilian brain), emotion (limbic brain), and attention (cortex).

Emotional states can be formed without consciousness: when you feel a strong drive to behave in a certain way, perhaps to overeat or to yell furiously at a stranger, it is more than likely that the reptilian and limbic regions have teamed up to push you to act. The linking of these parts of the brain with the cortex brings awareness to our inner feelings and behavior—for example, "Maybe I'm overeating because I'm anxious." Or "I think I should step back and take a few deep breaths."

The outer layer of the brain is the cortex. It is here where ideas and concepts are formed, where we think and imagine. It is where our five senses—knowledge of the outer world—are created. The middle of the cortex creates links to the other areas, including the limbic and reptilian brains and body. Language, the hallmark of the cortex, has unparalleled integrative qualities. The creating and retelling of a story requires the combined efforts of all parts of the triune brain.

All information from the body, limbic region, and brain stem—such as heart rate, shallowness or depth of breath, muscle tension, emotional state, and physical sensations—stream to the cortex, informing it of our "state of mind." When we block our awareness of feelings, their effect is still felt. Input from our internal world, with or without consciousness, continuously affects our ability to reason and make decisions.

Theory to Practice

In order to consider the ways in which the dramatic circumstance process stimulates various aspects of brain function—and vice versa—let's consider the work that Shane was doing in his coaching of "And They're Off."

Shane's first idea was that he was going to share information about his childhood with his girlfriend in order to get closer to her. By choosing an "as if" in which his girlfriend was his other, Shane was automatically activating the connections in his limbic system: that "primary area of emotional and social behavior." Shane has access to his feelings and the meaning of his relationship with his girlfriend because those connections have been made previously. They are now available to him simply because he brings his girlfriend into the story. There are actual neural pathways in his brain that are activated when he thinks of his girlfriend. This is why "as if" work can have such a strong impact on what a performer is doing. If you think of your story as if your other is someone significant in your life, present or past, you will be making use of those connections.

Shane's idea, however, that he would just share information with his girlfriend so that they would feel closer to each other was not a choice that was going to be supported by what actually happens in the song. "And They're Off" is a song in which the teller of the story gets more and more agitated. More importantly, from the perspective of a potent dramatic circumstance, there was nothing about that choice that put Shane at any risk. When he began to think, "What if my girlfriend wanted to meet my parents?" his involvement in his story grew instantly stronger, because Shane recognized that situation as being potentially dangerous. Dangerous, in this context, does not have to mean something bad. It is simply a change in the status quo that is sufficiently unsettling as to be perceived at some level as a threat, and the minute Shane introduced that "what if" into his story, he activated his reptilian brain. The thought of losing his fiancée, combined with his trepidation about revisiting traumatic experiences as a child by telling the stories of the ongoing struggle between his parents, engaged Shane's more primal sense of need and survival. Your "what ifs'" will always become more serious as they become more primal, and your need to take action will become more compelling.

Remember that the reptilian system responds to whatever danger it perceives regardless of the real nature of that threat. Anything that upsets the smooth functioning of the mechanism is, as far as the reptilian brain is concerned, a threat. That could be someone ending a relationship, or it could just as easily be someone realizing that he is falling in love. Your reptilian brain "constantly scans for danger," and it does not take much to get it aroused. When the reptilian brain is aroused, our nervous systems are activated, and both our limbic and cognitive systems begin to evaluate the nature of the threat. Shane, as a result of that engagement of these brain systems, immediately became more present in our conversation—more engaged in the story we were exploring and less aware of being in front of a room full of people.

Then we increased the level of threat. Shane's girlfriend became his fiancée, and the fact that he did not want her to meet his father was actually putting their relationship at risk. She made Shane's relationship with his father a "deal breaker" in the planning of their future together, and there is no doubt that Shane's reptilian and limbic systems were engaged. Keep in mind that the subconscious mind does not know that this is make-believe. There is no actual threat, and Shane has a perfectly fine relationship with both his father and his fiancée, to whom, by the way, he is now happily married.

The further Shane went into his story, the stronger the emotional connection became. This will be true every time he "tells" this story in order to sing this song, and the sense of emotional connection will both grow and evolve.

As Marcia tells us, the limbic brain organizes "sensory impressions into events: explicit memory." Shane's story triggered memories of connection, disconnection, family strife—all things that began to influence his behavior in response to living within this circumstance. The imaginary circumstance tapped into actual memories and emotions.

Most animals in danger or under stress, including humans, will choose the flight option over the fight option whenever flight is at all possible. Actors, however, occupy circumstances where they are forced to face the things that they fear. The character in Shane's position chooses to protect his relationship with his fiancée rather than to protect himself from painful memories. That, in fact, is what makes the story dramatic and makes it something that an audience wants to experience. It is unusual to see someone face danger head on. We are interested in that, and we are inspired by that. But at the point when a character is facing that danger, it is the more primitive brain systems that are providing the fuel. The cognitive brain may be directing the operation, but the limbic and reptilian brains are calling the shots.

We tend to believe that the cognitive brain is always our salvation. It is certainly what makes us uniquely human, and its power to think and reason has certainly led to our dominion over this planet. However, the authors of *A General Theory of Love* propose that it is our neglect of the limbic system and our lack of respect for the essential role it plays in our lives that is at the root of many of the psychological and sociological problems we face in our world today. The limbic brain is where we feel. It is where we experience empathy and recognize what another person is thinking or feeling. It is also, I believe, the part of the brain that actors engage in order to establish an emotional connection to a circumstance they are imagining as real.

Give It a Try

Imagine that you are going to sing a lullaby. If you are merely singing softly and sweetly, there is not going to be much happening that is of any interest to the listener—or, for that matter, to you. It may be pretty, but it will not be alive. It may put the baby to sleep, but that's not the response you are looking for from your audience. So if you imagine singing that lullaby to an actual child and take the time to really envision that child, your singing will change. You will have a scene starting to come to life. It will come to life in even more detail if you proceed "as if" you were singing to a child you really know.

If you go a step further and imagine that the child is just recovering from a serious illness, your singing will change further still. If you imagine the child has just been injured and is in danger of dying, your singing will change yet again. You do not have to change your behavior. You simply have to change your thoughts. The change in thought will bring about a change in your voice, in the actions you take, in the way you express yourself musically, and in your experience of a true emotional connection to both the circumstance and the child. This is acting. This is engaging the mind in play.

Does It Matter?

At the end of the day, any performance is as good as your audience perceives it to be. What you know and what your audience knows are two different things. That being said, in my experience audiences recognize the truth when they hear it and see it, and you will certainly always know if you are behaving truthfully within your imaginary circumstances.

Brain science is an important and ever-growing field of study that endeavors to address any number of mental, emotional, and physical issues that trouble many individuals in our society. Applying its principles to the study of acting may appear a bit frivolous. However, I think that the best actors tell stories about what it is like to be human, and I think that we as a society are better off because these stories get told. It only follows that the stories will have an even greater impact when they are told honestly and with true insight into human consciousness and behavior.

The dramatic circumstance process does have a significant impact on the way I see singers and actors tell their stories, and I think that brain science offers an intriguing insight into why the process works. It is certainly worth considering, and I look forward to spending more time exploring all of the systems and connections that allow performers to bring themselves more fully to their work.

15

A New Paradigm

In the university I attended as an undergraduate, the theatre department and the music department were in separate buildings that sat some thirty yards apart. They may as well have been on opposite sides of the earth. Music majors had little access to the theatre department, and theatre majors had virtually no access to the music department. Those of us interested in both music and theatre were left to our own devices. In the summers, the music and theatre departments would collaborate on a musical, but that collaboration usually devolved into a cross-departmental argument about whether the lead roles should be played by the student who could "really sing" the part or the student who could "really act" the part. The idea that the students might be capable of doing both things at the same time—if, in fact, anyone were training them to do both things at the same time—was really never part of the conversation.

After spending two years as a music major who would steal over to the theatre department to take acting classes and perform in shows, I figured out that I could most easily pursue both singing and acting by changing my major to psychology. That way neither department had control of my curriculum, my schedule, or my priorities. So that is what I did, and that is how I ended up with a bachelor's degree in psychology with minors in music and theatre. Even though this you-cannot-actually-get-a-job-doing-anything-with-this-degree degree seemed at the time to be the result of my indecision and an unwillingness to do anything that might lead to me actually getting a job, it later turned out to be an accurate predictor of the very path of my life and the very foundation of my career in the theatre. I have made my living for the past forty years as a "student" of human behavior (psychology), and I work every day to translate that behavior—whether I am teaching, directing, or writing—into actions that inspire speaking (theatre) and singing (music).

However, and as is so often the case, it is only in hindsight that I appear to have known what I was doing when it came to my college studies. The divide between the music department and the theatre department, not to mention the circuitous route I had to follow through the "psych" department in order to be able to pursue the things I wanted to pursue, was often frustrating. I was left to put together pieces of a puzzle with no guidance or practical information or even a clear idea of what the finished "puzzle" might look like. I managed to piece together some good ideas that helped me progress and some not-so-good ideas that really got in the way of my work and the career I wanted to pursue.

As someone with a real interest and driving passion for music theatre, I do not think that my experience was unusual. Unfortunately, I think it is still not unusual for many students today.

Even universities and professional schools that purport to espouse the triple-threat approach to music theatre study—all singing, all acting, all dancing—most often have faculty who have had little training or practical experience outside their own disciplines. These teachers do not put things together because they have never actually done it themselves, or in most instances, they are not given the time and resources they would need in order to show their students how to do it. Courses in "putting it together" are hard to come by.

For those performers who are not in school programs but are studying privately with individual teachers, the situation is often worse, and they are likely to be confronted by the fact that whenever information from different teachers seems to conflict or is inconsistent, they are left to their own devices to sort it out. More problematically, they can be forced to choose to follow one set of instructions while keeping that choice a secret from their other teachers. I know of many instances, including professional productions at the highest level, where singers were subjected to a barrage of criticism from a voice teacher once the teacher actually saw—or, more specifically, heard—the show in which they were performing.

It all boils down to the fact that in too many instances in too many arenas of study, music theatre performers are left trying to serve too many masters at the same time. They end up confused, frustrated, and performing at levels well below their potential. That is not good.

For practical purposes, performance studies are usually divided into three broad categories: singing skills, acting skills, and dancing skills. This is true not only in most schools but also in the "real" world, as those of us in the performance industry so often refer to it. These three areas of study obviously correspond to the specific disciplines in which teachers have studied and/or performed—those disciplines in which we hope they have acquired the expertise that qualifies them to be teachers. But in many instances the singing teacher has never studied acting, and the acting teacher has never studied music. And very few singing and acting teachers have ever studied dance.

It has been my experience, as both a student and a teacher, that those who teach singing and those who teach acting too often relate to each other as opponents in an ongoing struggle for the hearts and souls of the students they teach. To be more precise, they relate to each other as opponents when, and if, they choose to relate to each other *at all*. The inevitability of conflict between the singing teacher and the acting teacher is part of the conventional wisdom of both our schools and our industry at large. It is what everyone has come to expect. Voice teachers and acting teachers are each suspicious that the other is working within a set of immutable expectations and priorities that they fear will undermine, if not totally undo, the very thing that they are trying to get their students to achieve. For that matter, voice teachers tend not to trust other voice teachers, and acting teachers tend not to trust other acting teachers. It can be something of a snake pit.

Just what is it that they fear? Voice teachers fear that the acting process is going to interfere with the technical function of the voice, and acting teachers fear that singers are being taught to follow a list of rules that must be adhered to at all times and at all costs—that cost often being the truthful expression of a human experience. These fears are not unfounded and, unfortunately, have often been reinforced by actual experience.

It is not uncommon, particularly with young performers, for a wholehearted commitment to the pursuit of an objective to inspire a kind of physical recklessness that may not only impair vocal production but also actually lead to vocal damage. With some acting teachers, such recklessness is even encouraged. I was a guest director at a well-known conservatory of music where students in a particular acting class were proudly reporting that some members of the class were so "committed" to their work that they sometimes had to run out of the room in order to throw up. That cannot have been good for their voices. It was celebrated as "Letting go!" and "Breaking free!" A student caught up in the physical rush of overexertion will triumphantly declare, "I just didn't think about anything!" Thus, the idea gets planted that *thoughtlessness* is actually a way of working, that giving no thought to the way you are utilizing your voice and body is an acting technique unto itself. This is a dangerous way for a singer to work—particularly one who hopes to have a career in the theatre performing eight shows a week. Even at the Broadway level, there are notable instances of singers who have given powerful, award-winning performances while doing irreparable damage to their voices, and often this damage was evident in the roles they played, or could not play, later in their careers. The work was powerful and brought them accolades, but was it worth the prices they paid?

On the flip side of the singing vs. acting coin, it is not uncommon for singers to become so obsessed with protecting the vocal process that they are unable, or unwilling, to explore what the particular vocal or physical expression of a particular character might turn out to be. Singers have been known to claim, citing the support and utilizing the vocabulary of their voice teachers, both a greater knowledge and a higher authority. That "authority" is intended to strip the acting teacher or director of the ability to lead the singer down any path of discovery—any path at all other than the one that keeps the singer literally and figuratively "upright" at all times. This kind of rigidity can quickly kill the creative process and usually leads at best to a lack of spontaneity and immediacy in the singer's work. It is too often the case that very good singers have been labeled in their performances as "stiff" or "wooden" when actually they were more than capable of occupying their roles with full physical and emotional commitment. They just needed someone to show them how to safely access the natural vocal and physical instincts that would bring their performances to life.

As an acting teacher and director, I will admit that if forced to choose between the two, I value truthful work over the sound a singer is making. Fortunately, experience has taught me that I rarely have to make that choice. If any acting teacher or director is an active proponent of the singing-does-not-really-matter-if-the-work-is-honest school of acting, that teacher/director needs to recognize that this philosophy may well impair a singer's ability to ever find the optimal vocal function that will best support and illuminate the very truth the teacher is seeking in the first place. In addition, and more importantly, this kind of thinking invites behavior that could lead to serious vocal damage.

Teachers can understandably become territorial around their specific areas of expertise. Their knowledge is hard won, and their desire to help their students is sincere. I have observed this territorial behavior in myself. In a workshop I taught recently, a student reported to me what his voice teacher had said about the particular qualities his character should have and the emotional journey his character should be taking. I found that my eyes began to narrow suspiciously, and even though I did not say the words out loud, the student could certainly tell that in my opinion, this voice teacher was treading on dangerous ground.

When you get right down to it, acting teachers and voice teachers are in fact different creatures, and it must be acknowledged that the perpetuation of this age-old voice teacher vs. acting teacher conflict is not wholly their fault. A lack of constructive communication and interaction between teachers of different disciplines is the understandable product of the way most schools and universities are structured. For the most part, singing is taught in schools, departments, and studios that are run by musicians, and acting is taught in schools, departments, and studios that are run by actors and directors. In many schools, students who define themselves as singers are given little, if any, practical training in the art of acting. Students who define themselves as actors are often relegated to studying with "secondary" voice faculty or graduate assistants. I mean to cast no aspersions of the teaching ability of either secondary faculty or graduate assistants, but the fact of the matter is that most schools of music have a hierarchy of teachers. The students identified as actors are considered not to be serious singers and therefore not to be worthy of studying with upper-echelon voice faculty. The graduates of these schools then go out into the world where they themselves perpetuate this never-the-twain-shall-meet paradigm that then infects our profession as a whole.

We are caught up in a system that provides little to no opportunity for interaction or communication between teachers of various disciplines. It is an outmoded pedagogical model that, unfortunately, given the way that most schools are organized and administrated, is unlikely to change in the foreseeable future. And do not even get me started on the music professors who think that music theatre students are not really singing and the theatre professors who think that music theatre students are not really acting. That is another book unto itself.

Who is it that suffers as a result of this outmoded model for teaching and learning? I think we all do. I think our industry does. But most importantly, I think that those who suffer the most are those performers who are committed to working truthfully and want so much to act and sing *at the same time*.

In more progressive environments, you may be able to find teachers who agree that some level of "compromise" is, if not desirable, at least tolerable. But singers and actors are artists, and experience teaches me that singers and actors strive to practice their art at the highest level of expression. Do they really want—or do we really want—compromise to be part of the vocabulary of their work?

Voice teachers and acting teachers alike work from a base of knowledge that they have acquired over many years of study and practice. They work hard, and they take their work seriously, and I can honestly say that I have never encountered a teacher who did not care greatly about his or her students and the work they were doing.

There must, of course, be common-sense boundaries in place that are the product of each teacher's understanding of and respect for the differences in the things that they know and the things their colleagues know, and I am certainly not suggesting that the answer to our acting vs. singing conundrum is simply a matter of opening the floodgates and encouraging teachers to express their opinions regardless of their training, experience, or expertise. I believe it is, however, essential to the life of our industry that teachers explore new ways to work together. Students of singing and acting need to find new ways to integrate the components of their craft, and this will only come about if teachers are willing to talk to each other, listen to each other, and work together for the common good of their students.

I do believe that in the Vocal Performance Program in the Steinhardt School, my colleagues and I have found a different way of looking at singing and acting that brings together what so many people so often think are two conflicting fields of study. We have done that by talking to, listening to, and working with each other. That was probably the strongest motivating force in my deciding to write this book. I want students of acting and singing to be able to bring the components of their craft into a unified whole. I know that is possible. And I think it would be a lot easier, and much more possible, if acting teachers and singing teachers could work together to find a common vocabulary and approach that would benefit not only students but also our industry as a whole.

How do we go about this? Well, a little humility wouldn't hurt. In the early days of my teaching career, a singing teacher once said to me, "We wait until the song is learned, and then we put in the emotion." I asked if I could come observe a lesson when emotion was being "installed." The conversation deteriorated from there. I used to think this exchange revealed the singing teacher's ignorance of the acting process, and in fact, I still think that. However, I know now that this encounter revealed my ignorance as well. Working closely with singing teachers over the past decade, I have learned something that has had a profound impact on the way I think about, talk about, and teach acting.

I have learned that the craft of any singer or actor who hopes to perform professionally can only be built on a foundation of a vocal instrument that is functioning both efficiently and effectively, and until that foundation is dependably and consistently in place, all other work will be at best compromised and at worst not even possible. At the same time I have learned that the work of the acting teacher does not have to be put in abeyance until the singing teacher says it is okay to move forward.

The primary difference in what I think of as the "old school" approach and what I hope might become the "new school" approach is that serious acting work can take place simultaneously with serious voice work. Good acting work can, in point of fact, enhance the process whereby the singer's vocal abilities will continue to grow. That premise lies at the heart of the dramatic circumstance process that I have outlined in this book. I am certainly not saying that it is the only way, but in an industry that is definitely challenged in its ability to help singers and actors integrate their work, I believe that this book provides an approach that works.

I would like to see all performance programs for singers and actors, and all teachers who work with singers and actors, come to understand what I have just said, and I would like to see all of them utilize that understanding as an underlying platform from which they offer students the benefit of their detailed knowledge in their specific areas of expertise.

That Being Said

In *The King and I*, Oscar Hammerstein II has his protagonist, Anna Leonowens, say to her classroom full of young children, "If you become a teacher, by your pupils you'll be taught." I think Oscar got that right, and the most important thing I have learned from my "pupils" is that there is not really anyone who can teach you to act or to sing. I think that there are teachers who can show you how to access your natural abilities, how to access your instinctive impulses to step into a story and bring it to life, and how to make use of the natural function of your vocal apparatus to express yourself effectively in speech and song. Further, I think there are teachers who can show you how to enhance those natural abilities through training and practice. The best teachers, and the teachers you want to find, are those who are able to truly see you and hear you. Those teachers will utilize what they see and hear to provide you with better access to your body, mind, and spirit—the three fundamental components that make up your instrument.

What does this mean? It means that a good teacher provides access to the instrument that is you. A good teacher shows you how your voice and body and brain can be trained to function at their optimum levels—or, as is more often the case, how they will function at their optimum levels if you will get out of their way and allow them to do so. A good teacher will show you that you are enough, that what you have inside you is a well of understanding of what life means to you and how you want to express yourself based on that meaning.

You already possess within you, regardless of your age or level of experience, the ability to sing and to act. What you need, and what you are most likely seeking, is practical information on how to best access those abilities. That information is out there. There are teachers who have that information for you. I hope you have found some of that information in the pages of this book.

The guidance that teachers offer as they watch you work is an essential part of your training as a singer and actor, and there is no doubt that the input and insight you get from your teachers is, as it always will be, of great value. I know of no professional performer who does not maintain an ongoing relationship with the coaches they have come to trust. However, the information that comes to you from a teacher is never going to be more valuable than your own understanding and articulation of what it is that you do. In fact, until instruction is internalized it will have almost no impact on your work, and until that work is internalized it will be of only intermittent value. There should be nothing more precious than your own knowledge of your instrument and the processes whereby you get that instrument to function when you want and how you want. You must become your own teacher, your own coach.

Does it help to have someone guide you? Of course it does.

Are both teacher and student enriched by sharing this work and providing each other with information and insight? Of course they are. Nevertheless, the ultimate goal of every teacher and every student should be to go their separate ways. A student no longer needing a teacher would, in fact, be the best measure of the success of the work they have done together. While this may be a somewhat unorthodox way of looking at the processes by which actors and singers acquire the skills they need to perform, it is certainly a way of thinking that gives the student the ultimate responsibility and, in the final analysis, a great deal of power. It is immensely satisfying for me to work with students and see them make the kinds of changes that give them a new experience of immediacy and freedom. But when those students get up in class the next time and begin in a place that is already immediate and free, it is not merely satisfying. It is thrilling.

In the April 8, 2013, edition of *The New Yorker*, there is a fascinating essay by the concert pianist Jeremy Denk: "Every Good Boy Does Fine." Mr. Denk articulates better than I ever could the ongoing nature of a professional performer's relationship with those who have contributed to that performer's ultimate ability to perform.

> There's a labyrinth of voices inside your head, a counterpoint of self-awareness and the remembered sayings of your guides and mentors, who don't always agree. Sometimes you wish you could go back and ask your teachers again to guide you; but up there onstage, exactly where they always wanted you to be, you must simply find your way. They have given all the help they can; the only person who can solve the labyrinth of yourself is you.

Taking It Personally

Many years ago, I directed a national tour of *West Side Story*. Because the show was playing large cities across the United States and Canada, the licensing contract required that the production receive a stamp of approval from someone designated by the Jerome Robbins estate as one of the official "overseers" of Robbins' work. We had been in rehearsal for about two weeks when the choreographer who had been assigned to our production arrived to take a look at what we had accomplished. For the purposes of the story I am telling, let's call him "Joe."

The producers, the choreographer, the music director, and I sat down with Joe in the rehearsal hall, and the cast performed several of the large numbers. We then took a short break, after which Joe called the cast back together and proceeded to rip them apart. He told them in great detail everything that was wrong with everything they were doing. He did not like the way they danced. He did not like the way they acted. He did not like the way they sang. Joe went on to say that in his opinion, they neither understood nor were committed to the kind of work that needed to be done in order to make a production of *West Side Story* worthy of being on the stage at all, let alone worthy of the Jerome Robbins stamp of approval.

I watched the actors and could see the impact Joe's words were having. Some of them were hurt. Some were angry. All were certainly disappointed. The upset and despair in the room were palpable, but even so it took Joe about fifteen minutes to notice what was so clear in the performers' faces and bodies. He stopped in mid-sentence and said, "Listen, folks. You can't take this personally. If you want to be in this business you're gonna have to learn not to take it personally."

Just what did Joe mean by "You can't take it personally"? He meant that if you are a person who wants to act, sing, and dance professionally, you must be willing to hear how bad you are while not allowing yourself to feel bad about hearing it.

You can't take it personally? I sat there asking myself, "How else are they supposed to take it?" Joe was talking about them—about their voices, about their bodies, about their work. He was speaking about their ability to do something they had worked hard at and loved to do. How in the world could that ever not be personal?

Joe went on to say, "This is a business. This is about the work. It's not about you. If you aren't tough enough to take it, you better get out now." These young performers were being told that if they wanted to have a career in "show business," they had to set their feelings aside, something that is virtually impossible to do. Feelings, in my experience, do not like being set aside. They may allow themselves to be suppressed, swallowed, or denied, but they will eventually make themselves known in some form or another. And when they do make themselves known, it is not going to be pleasant.

Why did Joe talk to the actors the way he did? I think that Joe talked the way he did because he needed to make sure that this production of *West Side Story* met the artistic standards of its creator. That was, in fact, the job he had been hired to do, and he believed that going about it in this abusive manner was the only way to get the job done. It is likely that Joe himself was talked to in that manner when he was a performer. As a well-trained dancer with years of experience, he was steeped in a culture that is notoriously abusive. In addition, he had spent many years working under Jerome Robbins, who in many people's opinion was the meanest man in the history of Broadway. If you have any doubt as to how difficult Jerome Robbins could be to work with, just take note of the fact that he—Jerome Robbins—was actually fired from the national tour of *Jerome Robbins' Broadway*.

Joe truly did believe that he was talking to these young performers only about their work. From the cast's perspective, however, he was talking to them about their worth. Joe's need to do his job was slamming up against their need to feel good about themselves, and the very real effort they were making. They would have, as they proved in the next few weeks of rehearsal, happily done anything he asked them. Somehow Joe thought that he needed to strip them of their self-esteem in order to get them to do that. There are, unfortunately, lots of "Joes" out there in the world.

Performers face a formidable amount of feedback that all too often takes the form of negative criticism, and there is no question that criticism of this nature can be destructive. It does not help anyone learn anything. It can actually bring the learning process to a halt. But how often is it the case that the person stripping away your self-esteem is not your director or your teacher—or someone designated by the Jerome Robbins estate—but actually you yourself? When a performer begins to internalize such criticism, as we are all wont to do, is when such negativity can become even more destructive. It can become debilitating.

Are you your most severe and unforgiving critic? If so, you are not alone. As a performer you study and work in a result-oriented profession, and there is certainly no arguing the fact that we live in a result-oriented culture. We love focusing on the product and have much less interest in the process. You, however, as a performer cannot afford to view things from that perspective. Your process *is* your work, and you have to trust that when you commit to your process your work will be not only the best it can be, but also more than acceptable in the industry of which you are a part.

Our natural desire to be "good" and get things "right" is compounded, I believe, by our culture's obsession with success and the narrow definition of success that is then applied to anyone making an effort. Americans are by and large much less interested in knowing what happened than in knowing who won, and our daily lives are inundated with images of the exceptional few who have made it to the top. Living in a country where everyone has, at least in theory, the opportunity to succeed has saddled so many people with an imperative to succeed, and the parameters of that success are not only laid out by our celebrity-driven culture but primarily determined by the amount of money a particular individual has managed to amass. "Was the movie good?" and "How much did it take in at the box office?" are not, no matter what the media would have you believe, the same question. And very seldom does anyone ask if the movie actually had something to say.

I find that our national obsession with success can be particularly troubling for the aspiring artist. A perfectly understandable desire to succeed coalesces with a wholehearted acceptance of our culture's narrow definition of success. This pairing gives birth to an ongoing struggle in which you, the artist, spend most of your time drawing unfavorable comparisons between yourself and some unrealistic, superficial, and often corrupt idea of winning. When you devote your time and energy to comparing yourself—or allowing yourself to be compared—to some arbitrary ideal, you will always come up short. You will always feel like less than what you should be, and nothing can be more restricting than that.

In writing this book, I have drawn upon my years of study and practice in order to define a simple, yet powerful, process that I believe will allow you to take charge of your work as a performer, thus revealing the very best of yourself.

You have undoubtedly experienced moments in your work when you are able to achieve a state of uninhibited physical and emotional expression. You are suddenly free, and in that freedom you suddenly see and know things more clearly and more truly than you did before. At the same time, I imagine you have experienced that a commitment to truth in your work, while often frustrating and sometimes frightening, can be liberating.

I have reached a point in my life and my career where I finally understand that my own artistic pursuits—my singing, my acting, my directing, my teaching, and my writing—have all been part of an underlying need to experience both freedom and truth. This means finding the truth of who I am, and the ability to express that truth without inhibition or self-criticism. That is why I have challenged myself throughout my life and career, as I continue to challenge myself now, to explore and articulate ways of working that empower the artist in you and the artist in myself.

Joe, in a word, was wrong. It is always personal. I will even go a step further than that.

If it's not personal, what's the point?

ACKNOWLEDGMENTS

I am grateful to many people for many things, and I want to acknowledge the roles some particularly generous individuals have played in the process of bringing this book out of my head and onto the page.

For asking me, "What do you want?" so many times that I finally realized that the question itself, and not only the answer, was really important: Leonard Peters.

For saying, "Yes, I'd be happy to read your manuscript," even when people at dinner parties don't have to do that sort of thing: Anne Depue.

For saying, "I would like to publish your book," and picking up the check for the coffee: John Cerullo.

For lending their expertise and making me look more like a real writer on the page than I probably deserve to: Jessica Burr and Joanna Dalin Sexton.

For allowing me to incorporate my fond memories of their voices and their stories into the telling of my own story: Sean Buhr, Charlotte Delaney, Melanie Field, Kevin Mueller, Shane O'Neill, Katerina Papacostas, and Joanne Shea.

For supplying some well-chosen words that were far better than the ones I was struggling to find: Daniel Coombs, Christina Vogric, Zachary Wagner, and Rachel Womble.

For bringing their diligent eyes to the manuscript when my own eyes would no longer focus: Stephanos Bacon, Joe Conceison, Emily Crowley, Kareem Elsamadicy, Victoria Graves, Dylan Landau, Dan Lawler, Emily Neuberger, Ian Pruneda, Christie Rotarius, and Paul Wilt.

For welcoming me into the world of academe, trusting me, and providing so many unique opportunities for me to learn and grow: Terry Astuto, Mary Brabeck, Lawrence Ferrara, Anne Marcus, and Beth Weitzman.

For being not only exceptional teachers but also the finest colleagues one could ever hope to have: Meg Bussert, Brian Gill, Dianna Heldman, MK Lawson, Michael Ricciardone, Frank Schiro, John Simpkins, and Grant Wenaus.

For providing invaluable information, thoughtful insight, and much more moral support than she actually realizes: Marcia Lesser.

For over thirty years of friendship, wisdom, and guidance—especially because it always started out as if we were just having lunch: Norma Biondo Woodward.

And for putting up with my singing even when they knew it wasn't very good: Bill, Joyce, and Wes Wesbrooks.

ABOUT THE AUTHOR

University training in psychology, music, and theatre set the
stage for **William Wesbrooks**' career in professional theatre,
which has spanned acting, singing, directing, playwriting, and
teaching. Since 2001 his work has been concentrated at New York
University, where he was asked to assume the directorship of the
Program in Vocal Performance at the Steinhardt School of Culture, Education, and Human Development. As a Music Associate
Professor he oversees a program that trains singers at the bachelor's,
master's, advanced certificate, and doctoral levels for careers as
both performing artists and teachers. His NYU directing credits
include *Carousel*, *The Most Happy Fella*, *Fiorello!*, *Candide*, *A Little
Night Music*, *110 in the Shade*, *Into the Woods*, *Ragtime*, *Jacques Brel
Is Alive and Well and Living in Paris*, *Hansel and Gretel*, *Hands
Across the Sea*, *Street Scene*, *The Pirates of Penzance*, and *The Merry
Widow* as well as the gala performance of *King David* at which the
authors—Alan Menken and Sir Tim Rice—were inducted into
NYU's Musical Theatre Hall of Fame.

Wesbrooks' professional directing credits include Tovah
Feldshuh's critically acclaimed off-Broadway play *Tallulah, Halle-
lujah!* (named by *USA Today* as one of the "Ten Best Productions"
of the year 2000), the off-Broadway premiere of *The Water Coolers*,
Gypsy starring Dolores Gray, and *Shenandoah* starring John Raitt.
He staged the musical numbers for Sarah Miles' one-woman show
Sheba and has directed national tours of *Brigadoon*, *Seven Brides
for Seven Brothers*, *The King and I*, *Meet Me in St. Louis*, *The Sound
of Music*, and *West Side Story*. Regional credits include *My Fair
Lady*, *Peter Pan*, *Private Lives*, *The Mikado*, *The Secret Garden*, *A

Wonderful Life, and *The Pirates of Penzance*. International credits include *My One and Only* starring Jodi Benson (Cologne, Berlin, Munich, Vienna) and *The Fantasticks* for the La Fenice theatre in Venice, Italy.

His first work as a playwright, *Before I Wake*, was awarded a CAPS Fellowship and a Ludwig Vogelstein Grant as well as a development grant from the Pilgrim Project. With composer Ronald Strauss, he cowrote the libretto for *Barbary Keep*, a ballad opera that received a 1994 development grant from the National Endowment for the Arts and was produced in the spring of 2001 as part of NYU's new works development project. In collaboration with composer/lyricist Maury Yeston, he wrote the book for *History Loves Company* and directed that show's world premiere in Chicago.

Wesbrooks is a member of the Dramatists Guild, the Stage Directors and Choreographers Society, and Actors' Equity Association. Raised in southern New Mexico under western skies, and having lived life in the Big Apple for the past forty years, he now happily, and more quietly, divides his time between New York City and his home in Santa Fe.